CW00361609

Palgrave Studies on Children and Development

There has been increased attention to children and development, and children's development, in international policy debates in recent years, reflected in the United Nations Convention on the Rights of the Child and the child-centred focus of United Nations' Millennium Development Goals. This is based first on the interests of children according to their human rights, and second, a recognition of the importance of children for societal development. However, despite this increasing focus on policies and programmes (and budgets) to support children, relatively little has been written to draw together the lessons of development policy and practice as well as research into children's development over the life-course. This series will start off with a mini series of 3 books from Young Lives, a unique 15-year longitudinal study of childhood poverty in developing countries. It will also incorporate other edited or single author volumes, from a range of disciplines, which relate to and reflect the work being done by Young Lives on children and development, but broaden debates into the wider childhood studies field. A particular strength will be the ability to bring together material that links issues from developed and developing countries, as they affect children. As such the series will present original and valuable new data for an important and growing field of scholarship.

More information about this series at
http://www.springer.com/series/14569

Pia Jolliffe

Learning, Migration and Intergenerational Relations

The Karen and the Gift of Education

Pia Jolliffe
University of Oxford
United Kingdom

Palgrave Studies on Children and Development
ISBN 978-1-137-57217-2 ISBN 978-1-137-57218-9 (eBook)
DOI 10.1057/978-1-137-57218-9

Library of Congress Control Number: 2016948417

Printed on acid-free paper

This Palgrave Macmillan imprint is published by Springer Nature
The registered company is Macmillan Publishers Ltd. London

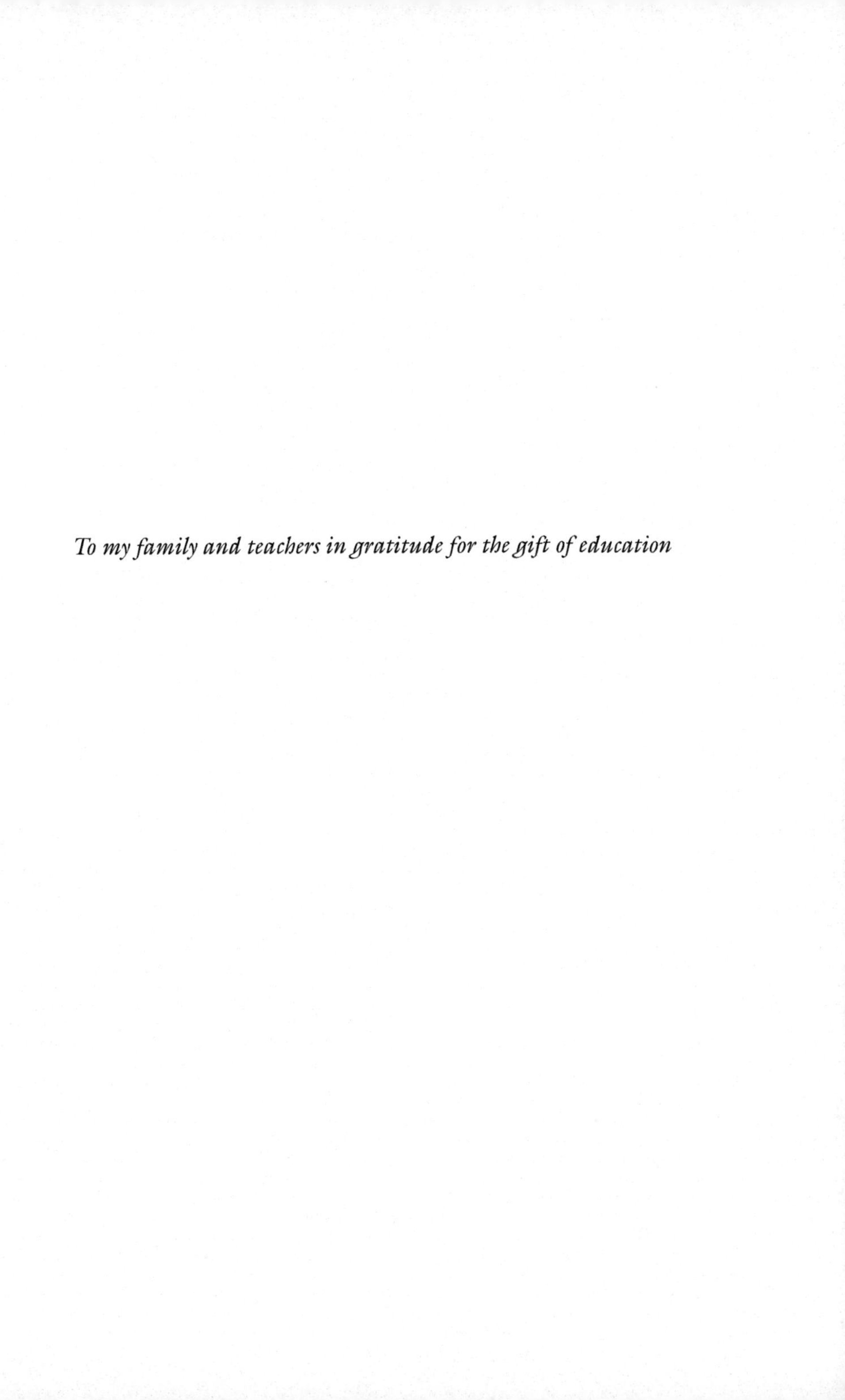

To my family and teachers in gratitude for the gift of education

FOREWORD

INTEGRATIVE LEARNING AND THE KAREN DIASPORA

Ethnographic research in low-income countries provides the kind of detailed and thick descriptive data needed for understanding educational processes and the role of education for quasi-literate minority populations in agricultural economies. Education is essential to stabilizing the lives of young people embedded in shattering traditional cultures, struggling to transition and adapt to life and work in the contemporary globalized and market-driven world. Field research can shed light on fruitful paths created by enterprising individuals working together in teaching teams. Research can help connect the educational process and outcomes to meaningful human development goals and to career opportunities within the context of local economic expansions tied to world markets. The research reported in the following chapters on the Karen refugees of Burma—now Myanmar—by Dr. Pia Jolliffe thus offers especially rich, compelling and poignant substantive data on the concrete challenges and issues faced specifically by a small group of Karen youth—real human beings—whose lives and identities have been destabilized by conflict, violence, displacement and their refugee status.

What do we mean by education in these contexts? Education always carries implicit if not explicit assumptions regarding power relations and the hegemony of the dominant culture, a tendency amplified in previously colonized regions. The classical dichotomy between techné and epistemé in education, dating back to Aristotle, is far more complex in the multivalent context of competing value systems and modern digital technology as these meet traditional structures of access to knowledge, challenging both local 'wisdom' and local 'practice'. Powerful vested interests are often aligned by class position with resilient patterns of domination, which results in blocked opportunities to access educational training in technical knowledge relevant to economic opportunities for minorities, such as the Karen, and for their geographic region. These same patterns of control and vested interests, according to many internationally recognized global scholars, such as Dr. Rev. Prof. Grace Davie, may legitimate the blocked access through local 'wisdom' or customs that support the status quo. These advantaged groups may actually seek to prevent the kind of human development among ethnic minorities, like the Karen, upon whom they depend for farming labour, to preserve existing arrangements of ethnic group power and control.

The patterns of dominant minority cultural deference and the transmission of these across generations are most clearly manifest in the Karen view of education as a 'gift', in Marcel Mauss' sense of the term, rather than as a right, a view more typical of a Western or United Nations lens. As Dr. Jolliffe notes in the case of the Karen, numerous interaction rituals symbolic of social distances are deployed to reinforce existing boundaries through symbols of deference and subjugation rather than professional employment and status attainment. The boundaries are ingrained early in the educational process and thus become all the more resistant to change, complementing the voluminous research on social class differences in education and authority in the West. Working-class parents value obedience; upper-class parents reward exploration and curiosity, differences amplified across indigenous rural and cosmopolitan urban populations.

Perhaps most revealing and touching in terms of cultural transmission are Dr. Jolliffe's descriptions of visits from benefactors. During a visit from Japanese donors, Karen children dressed in homespun traditional clothes served and performed in exchange for symbolic checks. For a Spanish delegation, the children approached seated benefactors on bent knees to present handwoven Karen bags. The ritualized gestures of subordination for the Karen children provide a sharp contrast to parallel rituals celebrating entitlement in preschool graduations among Western urban upper classes, where the children receive "diplomas" and are applauded by parents and peers as they take their first step onto the fast track toward an Ivy League degree and prestigious employment. The rituals symbolize and reinforce global patterns of domination.

The concept of cultural capital from the work of the French sociologist Pierre Bourdieu and its applications by Annette Lareau, recent President of the American Sociological Association, bear mention in this context. Lareau evaluated and then developed Bourdieu's generally accepted definition of cultural capital and his partitioning of cultural capital into 'skills', 'ability' and 'achievement'. Lareau accepts that dominant classes 'impose' evaluation standards. But then she shows how strategic interaction around agreed upon standards among parents from different social classes affects children's outcomes. Professional and middle-class parents effectively communicate both their compliance with institutional standards and their sense of educational entitlement. Her close observations, like those of Jolliffe, show real differences in skills at the micro-interaction level, with profound differences in outcomes for their children.

The work of Bourdieu and Lareau highlights the significant role of parents in educational success and status attainment for their offspring. Language is one piece of this and there are no easy answers. Whereas the failure to provide instruction in indigenous languages places students at a disadvantage and threatens the loss of entire cultures, the failure to ensure mastery of the dominant language ensures that the students will find themselves unequipped when they attempt to enter international markets. This is especially difficult with small, displaced minority groups such as the Karen.

Parental support for institutional standards, especially through strategic interaction in the dominant language and culture, facilitate status attainment. However, these strong ties, which shape core identities are especially problematic for marginalized ethnic groups. Language and traditional customs bind generations through processes of socialization, often, as Dr. Jolliffe notes, into gender-specific social roles. Just as these foster strong relationships between parent and child, they easily result in feelings of alienation from peers and from the demands of tasks and situations that challenge deeply held and felt traditional beliefs and practices. The alienation and sense of inferiority imposed by other children can further complicate and burden children such as the Karen, or, more tragically, can rob them of the supportive primary relationships that parents provide. In many parts of the world, such confused identities and the resulting resentment are a source of our most serious problems in the preservation of a peaceful world order.

There are no easy answers for the constraints on agency, save the development of a global teaching corps, trained in educational strategies designed to reach immigrant or indigenous marginalized groups in refugee camp settings, such as those described by Dr. Jolliffe. Especially important to the task are teaching models, such as John Dewey's, which emphasize transactional relationships between competent teachers and disenfranchised students as bedrock for democratic societies. Newer applications of integrative learning can help all students connect what they need to know as skills to meaningful life goals. And, like Lareau, Dr. Jolliffe notes the context-bound dynamics and significance of kinship and intergenerational relations in negotiating relationships with local institutions and authorities that can help them bridge relationships to international organizations with all-too-scarce educational resources.

In closing, Dr. Jolliffe touches on the motivation for Karen migration in their desire and need to access schools, colleges and universities, with brief comparisons of such opportunities in the USA and the UK. Immigration, assimilation into the new country and access to education are perhaps the most pressing issues in the contemporary world, as more and more children and families are displaced through violence, crime and wars. Comparative research, following the suggestion and thick descriptions from ethnography, such as that presented in the pages that follow by Dr. Jolliffe, thus offers an invaluable and evidence-based direction for future empirical research as well as applied educational strategies directed towards alleviating the struggles and pain of displaced populations.

Barbara R. Walters
City University of New York
USA

Map

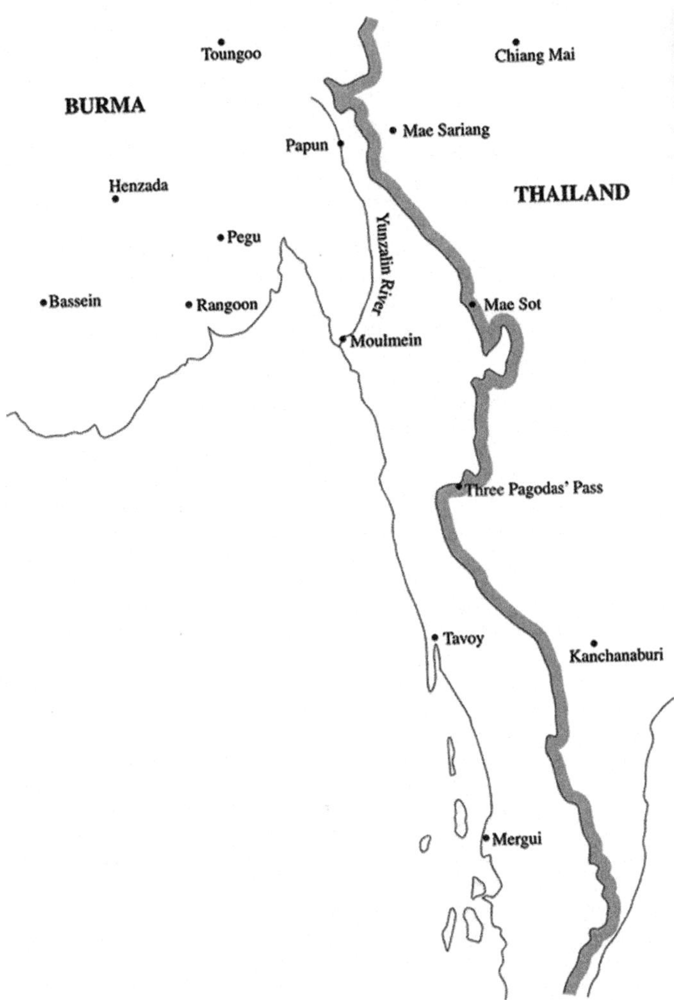

Map showing Karen locations in Burma and Thailand (Image courtesy of Yoko Hayami)

Acknowledgements

I have been working on this book for some time now and many people have contributed to it over the years. First of all, I wish to thank my academic teachers. When I was a student at the University of Geneva, Professor Philippe Régnier encouraged me to volunteer with the NGO WEAVE at the Thai-Burma border. At the University of Oxford, Professor Jo Boyden supervised my doctoral thesis on Karen childhood and youth transitions in northern Thailand. Jo's belief in the value of this research encouraged and challenged me throughout the various stations of researching and writing this book. During my time at Queen Elizabeth House, I also worked as research assistant for the Young Lives Project where I found much friendship and support of my research with the Karen. In particular, I wish to thank Gina Crivello, Virginia Morrow, Martin Woodhead, Laura Camfield, Karin Heissler and Elizabeth Cooper. Professor Barbara Harris-White, Jason Hart, Craig Jeffrey, Zarni and Benny Juliawan SJ challenged me to reflect upon the political economic shaping of society in general.

Next, I would like to thank Professor Sarah Harper and George Leeson for welcoming me as a research fellow at the Oxford Institute of Population Ageing. The stipendiary bursary during my time at the Institute allowed me to revisit fieldwork sites and develop the intergenerational dimension of this ethnography. Moreover I am grateful to a number of academic friends whose presence was helpful at various stages of research and book writing: Julia Amos, Anne Roehmer-Mahler, Mark Ebden, Susan Divald, Siobhan Burke, Chris Serpell, Jeff Crisp, Philip Kreager, Jacobus Hoffmann, Hafiz Khan, Melanie Channon, Emanuela Bianchera, Rose Metro, Kevin Fogg, Matthew Walton, Kirsten McConnachie, PJ Thum,

Benedict Rogers, Sr Eugenie, Phyllis Ferguson, Daniel Dolley, Claudia Azevedo, Julia M Puaschunder, Annette Goulden, Ulrike Gogela, Monika Rupp, Marcia Delves-Broughton, Patricia Simon, Veronica Sepùlveda Tornero OCD, David Townsend SJ, Simon Bishop SJ, D Matthew Baugh SJ, Timothy Radcliffe OP and Samuel Burke OP. Bridget Robinson proof-read most parts of this book's manuscript for me. I thank her, the series editors of Palgrave Childhood and Development Series and anonymous readers for offering advice on how to improve the manuscript. All remaining errors are, of course, mine. I am grateful to Linacre College for providing the space to exchange with academic colleagues over lunches and to Blackfriars Hall for accepting me as a Member of the Senior Common Room, where large parts of this manuscript have been written.

Next I would like to thank friends who helped me during ethnographic fieldwork for this book. First of all I am very grateful to the Karen people of Huay Tong village and in particular for my host mother Maliwan Kasedsookjai's warm welcome to her household. Prasert Trakansuphakon, Chumpol Maniratanavongsiri and Pierre Caset SCJ generously took time to explain Karen culture to me. Mitos Urgel, Jocelyn Lacierda and her husband Mie Tha La introduced me to education for forced migrants in and around refugee camps. At Chiang Mai University, Chayan Vaddhanaphuti, Malee Sittikreangkrai, Aranya Siriphon and Yos Santasombat welcomed me as academic host at the Regional Centre for Social Science and Sustainable Development (RCSD). In this respect I also gratefully acknowledge the Jesuit Seven Fountains Centre, where I worked in the Library during research stays in Chiang Mai. Vinai Boonlue SJ and Miguel Garaizabal SJ helped me better understand the working of the Jesuit Scholarship Programme for deprived Karen students. Naw Masu, Deborah Bourda and Alfonso Aguilera and the Karen students of the Arrupe Education Project were very helpful, too. In the UK, I am grateful to the Karen Community Association, especially Nant Bwa Bwa Phan and Win Cho Toe, for facilitating my research with Karen youth in Sheffield.

My family has been a strong source of support, in particular my parents, Franz and Maria Vogler, my sister Nora Vogler and her husband Armin Akhlaghpoor, as well as my grandparents, Hans and Emmi Vogler. From Austria, my grandmother Emmi followed my fieldwork on the map and my mother, Maria, even came to visit me and the Karen in Thailand. Last but not least, I thank my husband, William Jolliffe, for his love and support when working on this book whilst expecting the birth of our first son, Joseph.

Oxford, 2016

Contents

List of Figures

CHAPTER 1

Introduction

Around the world, schooling and other forms of education shape the lives of children and their communities. During her own school reunion, the Noble Peace Prize Laureate from Burma, Daw Aung San Suu Kyi, addressed her former school friends from the Methodist English High School in Rangoon in a speech emphasizing the communal and intergenerational aspect of education: 'Education is about to enable us to meet any challenge that life might throw at us, not just for ourselves but for those with whom we live. And those with whom we live are not just those in the family or town or country, but in this world today' (Daw Aung San Suu Kyi, transcript from video tape Methodist English High School, Burma Reunion 4th& 5th January 2013). As a matter of fact, the United Nations Millennium Development Goals are committed to improving access to primary education as an important means to promote gender equality and empower women. Indeed, in 2015 the primary school net enrolment rate in poor countries has reached 91 % and the literacy rate among youth aged 15–24 years has increased globally to 91 %. The gap between educated women and men has also narrowed (United Nations 2015: 4–5). In spite of this progress, many children are still excluded from formal education systems and those who access school feel they are not learning the skills they need for their adult lives (Department for International Development 2013: 4). According to the *Education for All Global Monitoring Report 2015* worldwide there were around 58 million children who were not attending school and around 100 million children who dropped out of primary school. Out-of-school children often come

P. Jolliffe, *Learning, Migration and Intergenerational Relations*,
DOI 10.1057/978-1-137-57218-9_1

from poor families and frequently live in conflict zones. As a consequence, many young people lack the formal skills they need for the white-collar jobs they aspire to have in the future. Therefore, within a global context of neoliberal markets and economic restructuring, it is increasingly necessary that the learning needs of children and young people as well as adults are met through equal access to learning programmes that encourage sociocultural skills (Banerjee and Duflo 2011: 74; Pells and Woodhead 2014: 42–44; UNESCO 2015: 110–111). This is particularly relevant in settings where increased aspirations for schooling impact on intergenerational relations, as parents invest in the education of their children and expect them to become bearers of knowledge and skills (Wagner 2015: 14). This book develops the interplay between learning, migration and intergenerational relations through the experiences of Karen boys and girls at different historical times and different geographical locations. The Karen value education as a gift that cannot be immediately reciprocated. As one research participant put it: 'I really believe in education. So, to give some education is a gift, priceless' (Nant Bwa Bwa Phan, interview, 10 April 2015). Anthropological theory questions the gratuitousness of a gift (Hendry and Underdown 2012: 65). In *Argonauts of the Western Pacific* (1922), Malinowski described how the economic system of the Trobriand Islanders is based on a system of gift exchange. Gifts included very big long shells, curved tusks and fine long necklaces. The opening gift of the exchange always has to be reciprocated by a counter-gift. Yet, just so these gifts do not end up as barter, the gift exchange requires that gifts are of different nature and also the passage of time between giving and returning a gift is mandatory. If a person is for a longer while not able to return a gift equivalent in value to the gift given, he can meanwhile use intermediary gifts of inferior value to fill in the gap. As soon as a gift of equivalent value has been returned the transaction of giving and receiving is concluded by a clinching gift (Malinowski 1922: 352–358). According to Mauss ([1]1925), the act of giving and receiving gifts tells about power relationships between two parties because 'the bond established between donor and recipient is too strong for both of them (...) the recipient puts himself in a position of dependence vis-à-vis the donor'. Yet the power relations thus established differ from markets: 'It is all a matter of etiquette, it is not like in the market where, objectively, and for a price, one takes something. Nothing is unimportant. Contracts, alliances, the passing of goods, the bonds created by these goods passing between those giving and receiving—this form of economic morality takes account of all this. The nature and intention of the contacting parties, the nature of the thing given, are all indivisible' (Mauss 1990: 76–77). In this study I suggest considering education as a non-material gift, because similar to material gift exchanges, education always engages people in permanent commitments, therefore creating and sustaining relationships between educators and pupils of different ages. This intergenerational dimension is important to understanding processes of giving and receiving education. Like other gifts, education cannot in most instances be reciprocated immediately. Time is needed to return the intellectual and practical benefits of learning. While this is often a question of years, sometimes it may only take hours for children to bring new knowledge home and cause change in the economy of the household. Conversely, when young people miss the chance to return what they received, they remain indebted towards their elders. In this case, the value of education as a priceless gift is called into question. This is particularly relevant for humanitarian aid in refugee situations (Harrell-Bond 1999) and in modern economies where young people increasingly migrate for secondary and tertiary education, but are left without meaningful employment (Boyden and Crivello 2014; Kabeer 2000: 473). The book also relates to a conceptual framework that recognizes that education is about different learning processes and learning contexts ranging from formal and highly structured settings (for example schools with professional teachers) to informal highly structured processes (for example government sponsored or non-state forms of education, such as independent school projects for refugees), formal unstructured processes (for example when children learn informally from their peers at school) and informal settings where learning takes place informally (for example transmission of sociocultural learning at home). Recognizing how these areas operate in interdependence allows us to discern how children not only learn at school, but also learn at home from their parents and grandparents. Such a framework is also sensitive to social dissonance during childhood.

Childhood and Sociopolitical Change

The various stages of the life course are shaped by cultural and sociopolitical contexts (Giddens and Sutton 2015: 346). In his *The Protestant Ethic and the "Spirit" of Capitalism* ([1]1905), Max Weber describes the individual's embeddedness into the structures of the capitalist economic order which 'forces on the individual, to the extent that he is caught up in the relationships of the "market", the norms of its economic activity' (Weber 2002: 13). Today's sociopolitical context of globalization is about the expansion of neoliberal markets and modern institutions throughout the world. Since the 1970s the flow of capital has increasingly disengaged from governmental restrictions. In the following years, circulation of capital and ideas across borders created new interdependencies and inequalities between northern and southern world regions. The local lives of citizens in poorer regions of the world have increasingly been linked to international markets, institutions and political developments (Harvey 2007: 89). For example, the pollution of water, often affects the world's poorest populations the most because they have no means to buy bottled water or move into areas safe from development-induced natural disaster (Francis 2015: 26). Social media may serve to critique or to support dominant political system (...) world communicate with their political representations outside as well as inside their home countries through the use of mobile phones and the internet (Green and Lockley 2012). On the other hand, nation-states may use social media to nationalism. For example, Huijsmans and lan (2015) evidence Huijsmans and Lan (2015) evidence how young peoples' everyday use of mobile phones is related to the forces of Vietnamese nationalism and the neoliberal market economy. Through the use of their mobile phones, young people willingly or unwillingly support these political economic power structures. Globalization therefore is not only about economic change, but also about the development of ideas, cultural and religious practices (Davie 2007: 206). Yet, Western theories of social change focus strongly on nation states, markets and modern institutions in a secularized world. They become problematic when engaging with the complexities of postcolonial settings or the ways in which global forces and culture are played out locally (Gaonkar 1999: 2; Ong 2006: 36). As a matter of fact, the formation of modern institutions outside Western Europe has not followed a similar dynamic, nor are modern institutions operating in a standard way around the world (Chakrabarty 2000: 14). Instead, everyday politics and the working of institutions may be shaped by archaic forms of culture or religion. For example, in her biography, Malala Yousafzai, the youngest ever recipient of the Nobel Peace Prize, describes how in the name of religion the Taliban undermined children and young peoples' access to school education. By the end of 2008, as many as 400 schools had been destroyed in her native Swat valley, and the government seemed to care little about the situation (Yousafzai 2013: 120). Similar stories have been told from other countries thus highlighting development economists' point that good politics need to be in place to guarantee good policies (Banerjee and Duflo 2011: 235–236).

The global and the local are therefore always relational. Accordingly, there is a 'simultaneous coexistence of social interrelations at all geographical scales, from the intimacy of the household to the wide space of trans global connections' (Massey 1994: 168). At the same time, cultural differences are increasingly deterritorialized because of increasing migration and exchanges between people, capital and ideas (Gupta and Ferguson 2001: 3). Therefore, global economic changes challenge the character of localities, as well as the identities and relationships between the different generations (Appadurai 1995: 41; Ong 2006: 5). Childhood transitions, in contexts of restructuring and globalization are often conceptualized as destabilizing processes. Many discussions on the impact of risk on children's development of a self-identity draw on the work of the psychologists Erikson and Winnicott in order to highlight the importance of stability and harmony in children's moral development. According to these theories, dissonance impacts negatively on identity formation causing low self-esteem, shame and other unpleasant feelings among children and youth (Beale-Spencer and Markstrom-Adams 1990: 301). This is particularly relevant for education in multi-ethnic classroom settings, such as in the Burmese migrant context in Thailand (Metro 2013). Also in my fieldwork settings, migration between institutional and geographic locations impacts on 'ethnicity'. The sociological concept of 'ethnicity refers to a type of social identity related to "decent and cultural differences" which become effective or active in certain social contexts' (Giddens and Sutton 2015: 677). Ethnic differences are learned and give meaning to ethnic groups as 'those human groups that entertain a subjective belief in their common descent because of similarities of physical type or of customs or both, or because of memories of colonization and migration' (Weber 2013: 389). Common language, ritual regulation of life and sharing of religious belief may be important but not necessary for the formation of ethnic groups. As a matter of fact, ethnic groups may distinguish themselves through language and religion as well as through material differences (for example economic activities, clothes, food or housing) and associated values of good and proper conduct, honour and dignity (Weber 2013: 391). As outlined later in this chapter, the Karen ethnicity has different meanings at different places. In my own fieldwork, Karen children referred to their 'Karen'-ethnicity differently depending on the geographic and institutional location. For example, they are proud to wear their ethnic clothes in their highland villages, but try to conceal their ethnicity when studying or working among mainstream Thai people in the lowlands. However, social dissonance and inability to keep 'fixed identities' does not necessarily affect children negatively. In fact, the modern emphasis on consonance often denies disagreement and minority opinions. As a consequence non-mainstream voices are frequently marginalized or silenced (Stone 1994: 51). Tan and Santhiram (2014), for instance, highlight the important role played by the Malay language in the nation-building process. The Education Act of 1961 consolidated the objective to make Malay the main medium of instruction at secondary school level, hence marginalizing mother tongue education of Chinese and Indians (Tan and Santhiram 2014: 60–61).

Sociopolitical change related to the neoliberal economy engenders conflicts around the world. As a consequence, thousands of children are growing up in war zones or refugee camps. Importantly, social studies show that children are resourceful in dealing with rupture and dissonance, even in extreme adversities such as war and natural disaster. Children's social agency and their ability to engage creatively with political economic forces that structure their everyday lives (Boyden and de Berry 2004; Mayall and Morrow 2011) are also acknowledged by social scientists. Writing against the widespread notion of 'the child' these studies underscore that power and status differences as well as gender issues, religious beliefs and political opinions, shape young persons' coping capacity in dealing with social risks (Chatty and Hundt 2005:178; Hart 2004: 168; Mann 2004: 16–17). At the same time, the literature cautions us to remain mindful of how structural constraints and migration shape young peoples' agency (Ansell and van Blerk 2007:27; Boyden 2013; Hart 2014). For example, schools can turn into locations where political, socioeconomic, gendered and religious stereotypes are reproduced, but also renegotiated (Anderson-Levitt 2003; Hart 2008: 24; Jeffrey and McDowell 2004: 132; Levinson et al. 1996, MacLeod 1987).

Education and Social Dissonance

Education and schooling are also about social dissonance. Around the world and throughout history, children and adults negotiated political, socioeconomic, gendered and religious relations in school compounds (Cooper 2014; Turner 2015). In spite of international initiatives such as Education for All, boys and girls continue to be affected by marginalization in education, because of differences in children's social status, gender, language, ethnicity and rural or urban locality (Somé 2012; UNESCO 2010: 9). Sometimes, schooling itself can foster social inequalities among children (Keyes 1991a; Vaddhanaphuti 1991: 153; Willis 1980). This is not surprising considering that modern educational systems historically emerged out of social change. In England and France, for instance, the process of industrialization and institutional secularization went hand in hand with the integration of education with the economy (Archer 1982: 11–13; Vaughan and Archer 1971: 2). The parallel between economic relations and the working of the educational system received particular attention from the sociologists Pierre Bourdieu and Jean Claude Passeron (1977). In their analysis of the French education system they even speak of an 'ideological function of the educational system', in the sense that schools effectively depend on and reproduce unequal social relations, whilst at the same time concealing this fact (Bourdieu and Passeron 1977:194–195). Bourdieu also explains how schools equip children with social and cultural capital necessary to negotiate their ways in life. His theory inspired other sociologists to analyse social inequality and schooling. Annette Lareau (1989) found that social status explains differences in parents' involvement in schooling. Her research highlights strong interinstitutional linkages between children's home and school cultures. Language, too, plays an important role in the fostering or challenging of social power configuration at school. Typically, the modern education system promotes national language, symbols and narratives. It is ubiquitous that state schools promote standardized languages as the national language. These, often artificially constructed standard languages, are usually imposed over regional dialects children may speak at home. Use of local language can then enhance or diminish socioeconomic and political status and participation within the wider geographic space of the nation (Watson 1994: 328–34; Williams 1996: 64). Ethnic minority children are considered particularly affected by social contexts marked by a plurality of values and norms. Dissonance may arise in settings of conflicting social values between ethnic communities and mainstream society and may cause low self-esteem, shame and other unpleasant feelings among children and youth. This is particularly relevant for education in multi-ethnic classroom settings where non-mainstream voices are frequently marginalized or silenced, for example through denying minority groups their rights to education in their mother tongue. Formal education may become a status symbol and create new social divisions, such as the distinction between 'the educated and developed' and the 'uneducated and superstitious'. In this way, schooling may serve as a means to integrate or assimilate minority groups into mainstream society (Jeffrey et al. 2008: 53; Skinner and Holland 1996: 282). This applies particularly to the lives of children growing up within a context of war and displacement. The role of education and learning in shaping young peoples' agency cannot be underestimated. Schooling and vocational training are likely to give meaning to young people growing up in settings of military and civil violence (Chatty and Hundt 2005: 176). Formal and informal learning can have a beneficial effect, especially during protracted crisis and refugee situations (Crisp et al. 2001). For example, teachers can provide psycho-social support for children in conflict zones and inform about important issues like first aid, landmines and malaria protection. In times of social upheaval education can also promote values that lead towards peace and reconciliation. Indeed around the world, parents continue to support their children's education in spite of structural constraints and unstable conditions in war zones, during flight or in exile (Magali Chelpi-den Hamer, Fresia and Lanoue 2010: 15–17; Demirdjian 2012: 9). At the same time, education systems are frequently complicit in conflict (Buckland 2006: 7). For example, Anderson ([1]1983) explained how colonial schools in Burma were instrumental in encouraging Burmese nationalism that favoured Buddhists as the dominant religious group (Anderson 2006: 119). Metro (2013) analysed history curricula revisions in Burma's multi-ethnic post-conflict society and found that these revisions can improve as well as worsen relations between ethnic groups. Whether or not education helps to unite previously separated groups depends on various factors such as the exacerbation of inter-ethnic tension caused by comparing contradictory textbooks, the danger of alienating smaller ethnic groups by emphasizing the most widely known conflict between the Burmese and the Karen—language barriers—the dominance of higher-status participants and fear of thinking critically as well as frictions caused by outsider's interventions (Metro 2013: 161).

Dissonance is also created between local realities and globally promoted consumer cultures (Katz 2004; Hart 2008: 20; Jeffrey, Jeffery and Jeffery 2008). The global cultural industry promotes images of successful lives based on prolonged schooling and subsequent entry into white-collar work. However, academic degrees do not automatically lead to employment. Governments and international donor organizations increasingly collaborate in improving the infrastructure and delivery of scholarships for widespread participation in education. But economic restructuring impacts severely on youth's opportunities to actualize these promises. Added to this are political-economic inequalities based on geographic locations. Especially in poor countries, young people may experience severe discrepancies in rising opportunities for access to education on the one hand, as well as the decreasing availability of attractive, well-paid employment on the other hand. In this way, new social divisions, such as the distinction between 'the educated and developed' and the 'uneducated and superstitious', may be created (Jeffrey, Jeffery and Jeffery 2008: 8). This book adds to this body of literature through the lens of Karen youth who migrate for education inside Burma and between Burma, Thailand and the UK.

Intergenerational Relations and Learning

Intergenerational relations are shaped by the cultural and sociopolitical contexts. The Hungarian-born sociologist Mannheim insisted on the social and historical embeddedness of 'age categories': 'the social phenomenon "generation" represents (…) a particular kind of identity of location, embracing related "age groups" embedded in a historical-social process' (Mannheim 1963: 382). In his view, 'generation' is more than a 'cohort' because it is defined by a shared worldview or a common frame of reference. Like social status differences, 'generation' shapes men and women's values and beliefs (Giddens and Sutton 2015: 346–347). For instance, in British and other European colonies 'youth' was a term that described the first generation of a significant number of those who received a European education. This education, in turn, distinguished them linguistically and culturally from their parents' and grandparents' generations (Anderson 2006: 119). Therefore sociopolitical change affects intergenerational relations. To be sure, in a changing political economy, social diversity among children and the elderly is increasing. In recent years, an increasing body of social research drew attentions to the effect of global changes and migration on local intergenerational relations. For example, intergenerational relations are affected by migration (Fischer 2015, Vanderbeck 2007). Migration research explored the role of remittances, rural-urban migration and the vulnerability of the elderly (Attias-Donfut and Waite 2012: 46–48; Schröder-Butterfill 2005) as well as multi-generational households and care for children and the elderly (Fischer 2014, van der Geest 2002). Sadly, age segregation, is also a consequence of many neoliberal societies where children and elderly are frequently marginalized if their needs do not correspond to market demands (Thang and Kaplan 2013: 246). Therefore, in parallel to the United Nations Convention of the Rights of the Child (CRC), there is globally an increasing support for the development of a Convention on the Rights of Older Persons (CROP) as protection against age discrimination (van Vliet 2011: 349). In the light of these developments, some theorists in Western countries and developing countries worried about the negative impact of socioeconomic development on intergenerational relations, in particular the abandonment of the elderly

(Aboderin 2004). Yet, social science research has shown that the effects of modernization and restructuring on intergenerational relations are more complex than often feared by popular media. For example, the work of Knodel et al. (2010) is a timely response to Thai mass media alarmist portrayals of elderly people who were left behind in rural communities after their children migrated for paid work to urban centres. In his paper 'Is Intergenerational Solidarity Really on the Decline', Knodel (2014) provides evidence of how adults and children adapt patterns of intergenerational solidarity to socioeconomic change. Also, Roy Huysmans' comparative study on elderly women in Laos and Thailand provides evidence of how changing modes of production in these countries cause a reconfiguration of intergenerational relations and care arrangements with grandmothers caring for their grandchildren whilst their adult children migrate for work to urban areas. Importantly, whether or not women in this study were perceived as 'elderly' depended on what they did rather than their biological age (Huijsmans 2013).

Therefore, intergenerational relations need to be integrated within a wider political economic context that pays attention to the interrelation of macro, meso and micro levels of society (Archer 2004: 138). At the micro-level, there are interpersonal relations through which one generation may or may not be supportive of their seniors and juniors. For example, spaces can turn into intergenerational contact zones that increase social inclusion and cohesiveness through the daily interactions of local people. Leng Leng Thang (2015), for instance, conducted fieldwork at a co-located playground and fitness station for older people in Singapore. In the course of her study, she found that the creation of these contact zones not only encouraged the parallel coexistence of the elderly and children, but also encouraged encounters between various ethnicities and cultures, as well as between citizens and foreign visitors to the city state of Singapore (Thang 2015: 28). At the meso level, intergenerational relations may be mediated by social institutions, like school, the workplace or church. In this respect, Hondagneu-Sotelo and Avila (1997) analysed 'transnational motherhood' as an example of how the market demands for female migrant labour to the US impact on mother-child relations.

At the macro-level, intergenerational relations are about how the political economy shapes the consideration that a given generation manifests consciously or unconsciously towards the past or the future of a political community (Anderson 2006: 6–7). Global economic restructuring urges the international community to reconsider their use of resources: 'Intergenerational solidarity is not optional, but rather a basic question of justice, since the world we have received also belongs to us' (Francis 2015: 78). In this respect, Puaschunder (2014) analyses intergenerational responsibility in the corporate world. Her research raises important questions about multinational transnational corporations and multinational enterprises' ability to perform intergenerational equity. It so happens that the neoliberal economy impacts on the quality of these interpersonal relationships and the reliance on the 'intergenerational contract' (Kabeer 2000: 456). Within the context of ageing societies, Harper (2006) identified three broad roles for families: as mechanisms for intergenerational support, intergenerational transfer and intergenerational solidarity (Harper 2006: 27–30). Of course, the extent to which parents and children look after each other at different phases of their life courses varies cross-culturally and is shaped by gender, socioeconomic status and household compositions (Goodman and Harper 2008: 8; Khan 2013: 321–323).

Learning and education are essential to intergenerational relations (Whitehead, Hashim and Iversen 2007: 28). Intergenerational learning has always been important and continues to be the centre of education in increasingly complex societies within a globalized world (Boyden 1993). Cross-culturally, children learn through guided participation. In this process, elders introduce younger ones gradually to the mastery of skills that allow them to assume increasing responsibility for managing situations and particular tasks. In this way, through their practical activities, boys and girls contribute as active agents to the transformation of cultural tools, practices and institutions that shape the historical and dynamic nature of community life (Rogoff 2003: 89). Importantly, intergenerational influences encompass more than biological caregivers, and may come from children's cultural interactions with parents, grandparents, aunts and uncles, teachers and other community members. Those adults with whom children spend the most time with—at home, at school, at play, etc.—may alter over the course of childhood (Vogler, Crivello and Woodhead 2008: 11).

Intergenerational learning is typically mutual and involves younger and older generations as givers and receivers of education. Indeed there is typically an element of reciprocity related to the exchange of knowledge and skills across generations. For children and youth this means a transfer of traditions, values, culture and life-time skills. Adults, too, learn from their children. In this way, they experience a transfer of new values, insights about traditions, changing social structures and new technology. Ideally, intergenerational learning is also about empowerment understood as 'an intentional on-going process centered in the local community involving mutual respect, critical reflection, caring and group participation through which people lacking an equal share of resources gain greater access to these resources' (Newman and Hatton-Yeo 2008: 33).

Intergenerational exchanges through educational programmes can be particularly relevant among migrants and refugees. Uprooted from their areas of origin, they need to find ways to adapt to modern education systems whilst passing on their cultural heritage. The transmission of language, in particular, is an important means to connect diasporas to the idea of belonging to one culture or a homeland (Chatty 2010: 302). Intergenerational learning also takes place at settings outside of school, such as informal school clubs and other institutions where education can be offered. This is also true for the Karen in this study who value formal education as a gift that they received, lost and found again.

The Karen

The notion 'Karen' in itself is a result of colonial ethnography, missionary activities and policies regarding ethnic minority groups in Thailand and Burma[1] (Hinton 1983; Keyes 2003: 210–211). In reality, the term 'Karen' includes around 20 subgroups of Karennic-speaking peoples. They are one of the many minority ethnic groups living in the hill regions of mainland Southeast Asia. The anthropologist Peter Hinton noted in his essay 'Do the Karen Really Exist?' how ten years after his fieldwork in northern Thailand 'it became increasingly clear to me that cultural features, regarded as essentially Karen, were shared by other linguistic groups. The importance of alleged ethnic boundaries had been grossly exaggerated' (Hinton 1983: 159). Indeed from colonial times onwards, anthropologists and other visitors to Burma tried to discern ethnic categories. For example, distinctive forms of textiles and dress were useful to distinguish and classify different groups. These labels may change over time and rarely reflect the complexity of local inter-group relationships. Moreover, they depend on whether it is cultural 'insiders' or 'outsiders' who are perceiving a piece of cloth. Therefore, outsider classifications are generally subjective and sometimes politically sensitive. What is perceived as 'traditional' cloth changes in colonial and postcolonial Burma (Sadan 2003: 170–173).

The Karen from Thailand and Burma

Until the mid-nineteenth century, Siam, the territory now known as Thailand, was composed of hundreds of principalities. Single political units were classified by local lords and places of residence, and not by territorial boundaries, nationality or 'ethnicity'. Accordingly, no spatial frontiers were communicated to others through political mapping. Instead of enforcing territorial claims, local lords requested peoples' labour as well as tribute in kind (Boonlue 2012: 22–23; Gravers 2012: 348; Hayami 2004: 46). These lords, in turn, were allied to supreme monarchs and elites in the ruling centres. Within this system, peripheral peoples were called *chao pa* ('wild forest people'). Although these peoples were considered of lower social status than those residing in the centres, they belonged as 'marginal subjects' to the realm of Siamese elites and northern princes and were closely interdependent with them. For example, local Karen chiefs paid tribute to the elites in Chiang Mai, who in return recognized the legitimacy of the Karen chiefs and granted them protection. Autonomy was an important characteristic of peripheral polities, such as the Karen chiefdom. For example, one chief could be loyal to different higher Thai authorities at the same time (Laungaramsri 2003: 23; Winichakul 1994: 8–82). This is in stark contrast to the centralized loyalty demanded by citizens in the modern Thai state, but typical for the flexible and rather egalitarian social structure among the non-state people who dwell in the region often referred to as 'Zomia' (Scott 2009: 18). In this way, the Karen and other groups maintained trade relations with lowland Thais. Through the mediation of these lowlanders, in turn, the Karen's economic activities were linked to the international trade system, which was dominated by European colonial powers. The Karen contributed to the wealth of Siamese rulers through taxation in kind, such as honey, hides and long peppers, and bartered these forest produce with Thais for cheap textiles. In the second half of the nineteenth century, these products were an important part of Siam's export goods on the global market (Platz 2003: 474; Renard 1980: 105–107).

This active and fairly autonomous political economic role of the Karen gradually decreased during the process of Siam's early state formation. Towards the end of the nineteenth century, Siam came into the involuntary position of acting as a 'buffer state' between Franco-British colonial powers in Burma, Indochina and Malaysia. Local rulers lost some of their lands and resources to British occupational forces, and it became increasingly obvious that non-territorial concepts of land boundaries were no longer useful. Between the mid-1880s and 1910, King Chulalongkorn implemented administrative centralization policies. Local rulers lost their status as territorial chiefs and were relegated to the status of salaried provincial administrators. Moreover, they had to give up their pre-colonial rights to extract labour and taxes in kind from their subjects (Hayami 2004: 49).

The construction of a new Thai national identity endorsed the administrative centralization processes. Bangkok elites adopted European pseudo-scientific notions of racial categorizations. In this process, Thai nationals came to be defined as persons who speak Thai and are loyal to the Thai nation. In order to prove the existence of this core or majority racial group, Siamese scholars started producing academic accounts of peoples at the national margins. They conceptualized these groups as (*kon pa*) 'wild forest men'. These *kon pa* were portrayed as 'wild', 'uncivilised' and 'strange'. They were contrasted with civilized Thais as the 'core' of the new nation state. A new distinction between 'civilised Thai' and 'uncivilised non-Thai' was thus applied to the spatial difference between people living in central areas and peripheral regions, such as the highlands (Laungaramsri 2001: 40). In 1956, citizenship was formalized in legislation. For the first time in history, a legal distinction was established between Thai and non-Thai citizens. Importantly, this distinction was based less on racialized categories and more on the political and strategic interest of space. Citizenship was accorded depending on peoples' location of residence and the strategic interest this location had for the Thai government and its political allies. In order to apply for citizenship, people needed to prove that they were born in Thailand. However, significant numbers of highland minority villages had not been recognized as national administrative hamlets. Consequently, people living in those areas were not eligible for citizenship. Indeed in the late 1950s, most highlanders were not registered as Thai citizens. Instead, they received 'hill tribe' identification cards that restricted the range of their mobility to their province of residence. The term 'hill tribe' was given official status in 1959, following the establishment of the Central Hill Tribe Committee to replace the Hill Tribe Welfare committee (Winichakul 1994: 170; Toyota 2005: 118). During the early 1970s, a range of Communist insurgencies in Thailand's borderlands caused serious security threats, which resulted in a popular stereotype of so-called hill tribe problems and justified increasing state encroachment on minority groups in the highlands. 'Hill tribes' were associated with issues perceived as a threat to national security, such as opium growth, undocumented migration and the existence of armed non-state actors. In this way, national security concerns were effectively linked to ethnicity (Laungaramsri 2001: 48). Since the 1980s, land conflicts between the Thai government and local villagers emerged and coincided with growing international awareness of 'ethnic' minority rights (Ganjanapan 1998: 202–222). In this context, access to modern education became increasingly important for the Karen to constructively negotiate with state authorities and international organizations (Santasombat 2004: 105–120; Walker 2001: 145–62). Scholarship support from the Catholic Church has enabled many Karen students to pursue their study at higher education levels. Some of them earned their doctoral degrees from leading universities and became key figures in promoting indigenous rights as well as in developing international networks on cultural rights movements. This resonates with the educational philosophy of Jacques Maritain who highlighted in *Education at the Crossroads* (1943) the role of education in developing critical thinking as a step towards emancipated citizenship: 'The essence of education does not consist in adapting a potential citizen to the condition and interactions of social life, but first in making a man, and by this very fact in preparing a citizen' (Maritain 1943: 15). In parallel, the Scottish philosopher Alasdair MacIntryre insists that education can only be successful when it develops children's ability to become reflective and independent members of their families and sociopolitical communities through the teaching of values related to the individual and common good (MacIntyre 2002). Thus, although ethnic minorities like the Karen continue to struggle within the Thai state school system, they also find ways to use the knowledge received in school for the benefit of their communities. Education has also played an essential role in the development of a Karen national movement in Burma (Keyes 1977: 56).

The border between the Karen State in Eastern Burma and the hills of the Karen in Western Thailand has only existed since 1890. At the time of writing this book, there were an estimated 400,000 Karen who were born and lived in Thailand and have Thai citizenship. The Karen in Burma live in Karen State, which is also called Kayin State or Kawthoolei, which can be translated as 'land of lilies' (Rajah 1990: 111) or 'a land without blemish' (Rogers 2004: 9). There exists a range of Karen groups such as Sgaw, Pwo and Pao. Of these, the majority are Buddhists (67–80 %), followed by Christians (15–30 %) and small minorities of animists and Muslims (UNHCR 2014a). During British colonial rule, the British favoured the Karen and offered them access to school education and government positions. Also, Christian missionaries brought schooling to the Karen thus laying the foundations for the development of a Karen national movement in the early twentieth century: 'The activism of the Christian missionaries among the Karen must be recognized as perhaps the most important factor in the development of a Karen national movement, a movement that has attracted many non-Christian Karen' (Keyes 1977: 56).

During the Second World War, the Burmese fought with the Japanese whilst the Karen remained loyal to the British. After the war the Karen were rewarded through large sums of money, Karen scholarships at Rangoon University, the building of a forty-bed hospital named after the famous English major Hugh Saegrim as well as a model farm (Falla 1991: 20–25). Notwithstanding these compensations, some argue that after the war once Burma became independent, the British abandoned their promises. In 1946, the Karen sent a 'Goodwill Mission' to London but returned to Burma 'empty-handed and betrayed' (Rogers 2012: 53). The Karen National Union was founded in 1947 and since 1949 the Karen have been engaged in armed conflict with the Burmese forces. Like other ethnic groups in Burma, the Karen have suffered throughout the decades of military regime. Many left their home country and found temporary shelter in Thailand. Because of the on-going conflict in this area, less than a quarter of Burma's Karen population live inside the Kayah State of Burma (Thawnghmung 2008: 4). In December 2014, the majority of the 110,607 'refugees'[2] in camps at the Thailand-Burma border were ethnic Karen (The Border Consortium 2014). In addition many of them have left the camps to settle in Thai villages and towns or migrated to third countries resettlement. Between 2005 and 2014 as many as 92,000 refugees from Burma participated in one of the world's largest resettlement programmes carried out by the United Nations High Commissioner for Refugees (UNHCR) and governments of third countries (UNHCR 2014b). The majority resettled in the USA; but Australia, the Scandinavian countries and the UK also participated in the programme to a lesser degree. After a few years the resettled refugees become eligible to apply for permanent residency and citizenship and many have already done so. In this way, the Karen are an example of a phenomenon of a growing number of today's exiled people who are not planning to return to their native homelands or to settle permanently in their first country of asylum. Instead, they aspire to migrate to places of greater safety, better education and employment opportunities and the possibility to reunite their families (Crisp 2014). These migrants, in turn, form the diasporas (van Hear 2009). In spite of political and economic changes, the Karen in Burma, Thailand and the UK share a cultural heritage, including respect for the value of education.

The Legend of the Lost Book

The introduction of Western education and schooling to the peoples of Burma, including the Karen, has historically been linked to Christian missionaries and British Empire building. However, the value of access to formal knowledge is enshrined in Karen mythology, especially in the legend of the lost book. Various versions of this legend also exist among other peoples in Southeast Asia, like the Kayah in Eastern Burma (Robinson, interview, 13 March 2015).

According to this legend, education is a gift that the Karen once received in the form of a golden and silver book from Y'wa. After they received the book, the Karen lost it to their younger 'white' brother. Animists, Buddhists and Christians interpreted the legend in different ways (Buadaeng 2008: 87). For example, whilst Christian missionaries often saw in Y'wa the biblical God, Charles Keyes (1977) cautions: 'The fact that missionaries were the first to record these myths has led to their interpretations coloring the understanding of them ever since. Y'wa cannot in fact be seen (at least prior to Christian missionization) as a high god that approximates the biblical concept of God. For the Karen, Y'wa represents a natural state, including the distinction between men, some of whom are literate and others of whom, like the Karen, are not' (Keyes 1977: 52). Also the 'white brother' and 'the book' have been interpreted in different ways. Theodore Stern (1968) explains how American Baptist missionaries readily accepted that some Karen saw in them the 'white brother' returned and in the bible the 'book of gold'. Alternatively, Karen members of the Tekakhon Buddhist sect jumble traditional Karen gods with the figure of the 'white brother'. These are moreover fused with conventional Buddhist beliefs around the figure of Ariya (Stern 1968: 316).

Until today, the legend of the lost book has been told and retold with various modifications, but in essence it explains an original injustice that caused the Karen to remain mostly engaged in subsistence farming whilst other peoples advanced in technology and knowledge. The legend became prominent during the Karen's encounters with nineteenth-century American Baptist missionaries who encouraged the Karen to associate the Bible with their 'lost book'.

During fieldwork in various Karen communities in Thailand, Burma and the UK, I recorded and analysed oral and written versions of the legend. I thus found two basic versions of the story of the Lost Book. The first version says the book fell into the hands of the 'white' foreigner (Phan 2009: 65). The second version says that the book was burned and the chicken ate the remains of it. During fieldwork in Thailand in 2015, Loo Shwe, a Karen refugee youth told me the legend in a way that combines both versions. According to Loo Shwe, God had three sons, the Karen, the Burmese and the English. One day the Father asked all three to bring food. The English son brought very delicious meat. The second brother brought fruit. Also the eldest brother, the Karen brought a tiny portion of food of a different, bitter sweet taste. God felt best after eating the food the Karen brought. So, God said: 'oh, you are the oldest and you are very clever. Bringing nice food'. When the God father returned to heaven, he asked the Karen to come with him, but he responded: 'I am not free. Because I have to work in the farm'. So, God asked the youngest English brother to come with him to heaven. There he gave him two books. We call it *Li Tu Li Si*. *Li tu* means golden book and *Li si* means silver book. But they mix it together. The books contained all the knowledge in the world. God said, give this book to your older brother and keep the second book. The youngest brother took both books and promised to return the book to his elder brother. However, when he returned to the farm, he showed to his oldest brother the book. But he was working in the farm. Therefore, the older brother put the book on a tree trunk and the younger brother returned to his house. And the older brother also went away and forgot the book on the tree trunk. After a while, the termites came and ate the book. And a hen came to eat the termites. When the Karen returned, he only saw chicken scratch remains. Therefore, in order to regain access to the knowledge of the book, the Karen killed the chicken and looked at the chicken bone as if it were a book containing important imformation. This is the reason why the Karen to this day use chicken bones for divination. In the meantime, the youngest brother returned to his place, read the book and learned a lot from it. The older Karen brother kept hoping that maybe one day the younger brother will return the knowledge to him (Loo Shwe, interview, 25 March 2015).

Also in the UK, Bwa Bwa Phan, eldest daughter of Padoh Mahn Sha Lah Phan, remembered in an interview how her school teachers in the Karen State of Burma taught the the legend of the lost book in class: 'It's a long time ago. All I remember is: We got a book. And the Karen brother was not looking after it properly and so it got missing. It got lost. So they believe that the white man is going to bring the book back later' (Phan, interview, 10 April 2015). In this way, the legend of the lost book highlights the symbolic value of education and the importance of time and space in knowledge transfer. The passing of time and the crossing of geographical distances foster intergenerational relations as well as social inequality related to the giving and receiving of knowledge. These power imbalances are not static. Time is needed to offer a gift as well as to return that gift through counter-services. Once former recipients of the gift of education reciprocate what they have received, a reconfiguration of social relationships takes place. Christian missionary education in Burma and Thailand highlights the profound meaning of the legend of the lost book. To this day, some Karen refer to the lost book in their encounters with Western missionaries and humanitarian aid workers and politicians (Rogers 2004: 211). Also in the accounts of other anthropologists, the legend of the lost book was presented as an important representation of the Karen self and other. It has been handed down by different generations of Karen in Burma as well as in Thailand (Hayami 2004: 25). The legend clearly distinguishes between formal education contained in the book and practical tasks that eventually lead towards agricultural work. The knowledge written down in the book seems to be the key to progress and socioeconomic development. Rather than chasing this knowledge, the Karen in the legend patiently wait for the gift of education to return to them. Of course, not all Karen perceive modern education naively as a gift that promises improvement of their lives. Indeed in spite of their access to school, the Karen remain in a marginalized position because the language of instruction at the schools they are attending is predominantly Burmese, Thai or English. Nevertheless Karen youth are not merely passive victims of a dominant school system of Western education. Instead, this book argues, Karen youth at different historical times and different geographical locations value formal education as a means to participate in intergenerational networks of households, markets and modern institutions at the local, national and transnational level.

Research Context and Methods

At the time of writing this book, I had met the Karen at different times and locations. What struck me about them wherever I went was their thirst for education and openness to learning new forms of knowledge that complemented their traditional ways of life. I met the Karen and other people from Burma for the first time in 2006 when I volunteered with a small non-governmental organization in Mae Hong Son. My task was to draft a curriculum for women's education in a refugee camp. For this purpose we regularly visited the camp and also met refugees outside the camp in Mae Hong Son. While most of these refugees were Karenni, some were Karen or had a Karen parent. Among the local and international humanitarian aid worker community I also met Karen who were born and raised in Thailand. Their cultural closeness with the Karen from Burma qualified them in a particular way for aid and relief work with Burma's displaced people. January 2006 was also when the Committee on the Rights of the Child (CRC) endorsed, in General Comment 7, children's right to education from birth (CRC 2006). At the same time, the United Nations High Commissioner for Refugees had launched a large scale resettlement programme to help refugees from Burma in Thailand to find a new home in third countries, principally in the USA but also others including the UK. It was also while volunteering in the small, hot office of the NGO that I received my own call to the UK: an email notification that offered me a place to study for a doctoral degree at Queen Elizabeth House (Department of International Development, University of Oxford). In my doctoral dissertation I decided to research the role of education and work among Karen children and youth. Therefor, I returned to Thailand in 2007. When searching for a good fieldwork site, the Jesuit priest Fr. Vinai Boonlue introduced me to his native village Huay Tong in the highlands of Chiang Mai. His own family, especially his sister Maliwan, welcomed me as a guest to their home. Thus, for a period of 12 months I stayed with this Karen family. They introduced me to other villagers and Thai teachers and soon I accompanied children as they migrated between households and villages to access education at Thai government schools. This gave me an opportunity to study children's educational migration and the power configurations that structured their home and school cultures, as well as children's agency in negotiating their working and learning lives. This research opened my eyes to the value formal education has in the eyes of Karen people. I realized that despite being rice farmers who live in rather remote areas in the hills of Thailand, the Karen have connected with the markets and modern institutions of their contemporary regional, national and global society. Education was key to accessing jobs in the labour market to supplement the little they earned through agriculture and market gardening. A cash income was necessary to pay for essentials such as medicine, school uniforms and transport. Cash income was also necessary to afford television, mobile phones, motorcycles and cars. Parents therefore invested in their children's education. When primary or secondary educations were not available in children's home villages, boys and girls migrated for education to other villages or towns. Karen children's educational migration has increased steadily since the 1990s. Of course, parents who invested in their children's education also expected something in return. And indeed today, more than in the past, young Karen adults are working in fields other than agriculture, such as teaching, humanitarian work, administrative work and nursing. At the same time, many Karen youth return to their mountain villages because they cannot find work despite their school certificates. Nevertheless, they still value education because it widens their horizon and allows them to participate in the modern economy.

I revisited the Karen in Thailand in December 2013 and March 2015. I also went to Huay Tong village and found that there were a group of Burmese Karen refugees temporarily resident in the village. This group of 18 youth had arrived in the refugee camps at the Thai-Burma border as teenagers. When I met them they had left the camps and were participating in a Jesuit education project. The aim of this project was to help Karen refugees to integrate in Thailand and to equip them with different skills for the next steps in their life course. Their situation was a stark reminder that over the last few years thousands of Karen youth had left their homes in Eastern Burma because of civil strife. A major reason for young peoples' displacement was often the lack of education. They heard about the refugee camps and migrant schools in and around refugee camps in Thailand and therefore crossed the border to access education. Aid agencies and individuals generously responded to refugee youth's thirst for education, yet, college or university education still seemed out of reach for most members of this generation. In spite of these structural constraints, Karen boys and girls in the Thai refugee camps felt they received a good education. And indeed from 2006 onwards some of the most qualified and best educated Karen participated in the UNHCR resettlement programme. In this way, 500 Karen of different generations arrived in the UK. At the time of writing this book, they lived in the areas of Sheffield and London. From January 2015 onwards I started visiting these Karen communities with my husband, William. In interviews I learned that the Karen children in the UK have been attending local state schools and many, in fact, have made the transition to college and university. It was through the encounters with

Karen refugees in Thailand and the UK that I started to develop the idea of a book that focuses on the value of education among different generations of Karen in various geographic locations.

This study combines historical and ethnographic research. The historical research has been conducted in the Bodleian Library (University of Oxford), the British Library (London) the Staatsbibliothek zu Berlin well as in private libraries of friends in Thailand and the UK. The ethnographic fieldwork has been carried out intermittingly between 2007 and 2015 in rural and urban areas in Thailand, the IDP village Etuta in Burma and the cities of Sheffield and London in the UK. Research methods involved participant observation (Spradley 1980) and semi-structured interviews with Karen children, young people and adults. In addition, I discussed in structured and semi-structured interviews (Kvale 1996) schooling, migration and intergenerational relations with many other persons such as teachers, academics, priests and religious sisters, as well as with humanitarian aid workers. Participatory research exercises (Boyden and Ennew 1997; Camfield, Crivello and Woodhead 2009; Laws, Harper and Marcus 2003) were conducted with groups of Thai-Karen children aged 11–15 years and Burmese-Karen youth aged 19–25 years. Moreover, in one high school in Chiang Mai, students of different ethnicity filled out worksheets sharing their experience of education at a Thai government school.

Ethical issues have been treated thoughtfully throughout the whole research process of fieldwork preparation, data gathering, analysis and representation of research findings. At all stages of my research, careful attention was paid to informed consent and confidentiality, power relations between me and others and data handling. I prepared an informed consent form in English with Thai translation. Throughout the research, I negotiated and renegotiated informed consent and made every effort to ensure confidentiality. Before actively engaging individuals in the research process, their consent was always established and I clarified the purpose of the research and the data use. The persistence of informed consent was verified on a continuous base. Similar to other researchers (Saunders, Kitzinger and Kitzinger 2015), I found the process of anonymizing data challenging because it involved balancing research participants' own views with the recommendations for good research practice set out by the British Sociological Association. Indeed, during the process of visual data generation, I suggested to young adult refugee research participants that they work with pseudonyms. However, the young people said they were fine using their real names; and some even signed their life course drawings very visibly with their real names. After several rounds of data analysis and discussion of my research findings at seminars and workshops, I decided to anonymize research participants' names so as to guard against unpredictable harmful consequences for research participants (British Sociological Association 2002: #26). I left the names of interview partners whose public work and care for the Karen refugees is known.

Throughout the whole research process I was sensitive to personal and institutional power relations along socioeconomic, political, gender and generational lines. Navigating these shifting power configurations demanded a great deal of empathy but also detachment from my side. In qualitative research, empathy is critical in gaining access to research participants' life worlds, value systems and patterns of reasoning: 'Knowledge is blind, empty, and restless, always pointing back to some kind of experienced, seen act. And the experience back to which knowledge of foreign experience points is called empathy' (Stein 1989: 19). In this way I tried to abate existing power relations between myself and the research participants as much as I could.

Book Structure

Writing about the role of education in the lives of individual Karen friends reminded me of Karen women who lift the warp threads on a simple handloom. This loom can be moved around and rolled up. Yet, its width is limited to the size of a quarter of a tunic. Therefore, to create a garment, many tunics have to be sewn together at the front, at the back and also under the arms. In a similar way, writing this book is about relating six substantive chapters to each other within a conceptual framework that views education through Mauss' concept of the gift.

Following this introductory Chaps. 1 and 2 is titled 'Sociocultural Learning' and argues that among the Karen people in Burma and northern Thailand, childhood transitions are about girls' and boys' increasing participation in sociocultural activities related to family work, and how these activities, in turn, are shaped by social transformations and rural development. The chapter also highlights how sociocultural learning fosters intergenerational relations and informs boys' and girls' life course aspirations.

The title of Chap. 3 is 'The Value of School'. This chapter critically examines schooling and formal education in the lives of the Karen in Burma and Thailand. Based on historical research, the chapter discusses the introduction of Western education through Christian missionaries in Burma and Thailand within a political-economic context of British Empire and modern nation-state building. The experience of the Karen in Thailand highlights how schooling enabled a whole generation of children to read and write, turning them into adults who value education and encourage their own children's rising aspirations for formal learning. At the same time, school remains a place where Karen children experience marginalization and discrimination.

Chapter 4, 'Schools as Sites of Inclusion and Marginalization', explores the impact of modern education on the Karen people in northern Thailand. The chapter explains the historical background of the Karen's marginalized position in Thailand and the role of education in encouraging their integration into the Thai body politic. Based on ethnographic fieldwork, I argue that the Karen value education as a means of sociopolitical integration and that they find ways to transmit their cultural heritage through school education. Moreover, the chapter shows that government schools are also sites where existing forms of marginalization are reinforced and new inequalities between the Karen and other peoples are created.

Chapter 5, 'Migration for Education and Social Inequality', focuses on scholarship programmes in support of needy students' access to formal education at Thai government schools. Although government education is free of charge in Thailand, many Karen children in the highlands of rural Thailand struggle to access education. Major obstacles include the costs of uniforms, school supplies and transportation across the geographical distance between children's households and schools. Based on ethnographic fieldwork, this chapter analyses the role of fosterage and intergenerational relations in structuring children's migration for education between highland villages and lowland towns. In addition, the chapter discusses how young peoples' migration for education shapes their sociocultural identities.

Chapter 6, 'Education and Displacement at the Thai-Burma Border', highlights the role of education within a context of internal displacement and refugee life in exile. Secondary and post-secondary education are largely absent in the former war zones of Eastern Burma. Therefore, young peoples' search for education caused many girls and boys to cross the border to Thailand where education was provided in refugee camps. Using the example of a Post Ten School the chapter draws attention to the challenges students and their teachers faced with regard to camp-based post-secondary education. The example of the Jesuit education project illustrates how small-scale education projects outside camps can foster young peoples' aspirations for post-secondary education whilst keeping them grounded in the reality of working lives and job searching within a context of intergenerational interdependencies and political economic constraints.

Chapter 7, 'Learning and Integration in the UK', analyses how Karen children and youth experienced the transition from refugee-camp-based education to education in British high schools, colleges and universities. Based on interviews with Karen youth in Sheffield, the chapter highlights young peoples' perceptions of how British schooling asked them to understand new ways of teacher-student relationships, teaching methods, peer relations and intergenerational relations between teachers and students as well as between young Karen people and their Karen parents. Based on their subjective experiences, students evaluate the advantages and disadvantages of the British school system and suggest how their education can be useful to support Karen educational projects in Burma.

Notes

1. Birmânia was the name given around 500 years ago by mainly Portuguese Westerners to the land between the territories of Arakan, Mons and Bama (Myint Swe 2014: ix). The British also used the name 'Burma' when they annexed the region through the three Anglo-Burmese wars of the 19th century. In 1989, the military regime changed the country's name to 'Myanmar'. At the time of writing this book, this was also the name with which the international system used to refer to the country. In the Burmese language, the country is called *myanma* in formal contexts, while it is often called *bama* in conversation (Metro 2011: 9). 'Myanmar' was, at the time of writing this book, the name officially used by the United Nations. I decided to use the name Burma as this is the name all my research participants used. Significantly, research participants have been of different age groups, ethnic, religious and social status. Since 2006 I met them at different moments and locations in Burma, Thailand and the UK. Throughout this exchange, none of them ever used the name 'Myanmar'. Instead everyone referred to their homeland as 'Burma'. It is out of respect to my research participants that I shall do likewise.
2. Thailand is not a signatory to the 1951 Convention of Refugees and its 1967 Protocol. Nevertheless, all those who fled from Burma to Thailand are subject to the principle of humanitarian *non-refoulement*, which extends to all people displaced by armed conflict independent of the standards set by the 1951 Convention (Moore 2014).

Bibliography

Aboderin, I. 2004. Modernisation and Ageing Theory Revisited: Current Explanations of Recent Developing World and Historical Western Shifts in Material Family Support for Older People. *Ageing and Society* 24(1): 29–50.

Anderson, B. 2006. *Imagined communities.* London: Verso.

Anderson-Levitt, K.M. 2003. A world culture of schooling? In *Local meanings, global schooling: Anthropology and world culture today*, ed. K.M. Anderson-Levitt, 1–26. New York: Palgrave Macmillian.

Ansell, N., and L. van Blerk. 2007. Doing and belonging: Toward a more than-representational account of young migrant identities in Lesotho and Malawi. In *Global perspectives on rural childhood and youth*, ed. R. Panelli, S. Punch, and E. Robson, 17–28. New York: Routledge.

Appadurai, A. 1995. The production of locality. In *Counterworks: Managing the diversity of knowledge*, ed. R. Fardon, 204–226. London: Routledge.

Archer, M.S. 1982. *The sociology of educational expansion: Take-off, growth and inflation in educational systems.* London: Sage.

Archer, M.S. 2004. Family concerns and inter-generational solidarity. In *Intergenerational solidarity, welfare and human ecology*, ed. Mary Ann Glendon, 122–152. Vatican City: Pontifical Academy of Social Sciences.

Attias-Donfut, C., and L. Waite. 2012. From generation to generation: Changing family relations, citizenship and belonging. In *Citizenship, belonging and intergenerational relations in African migration*, ed. C. Attias-Donfut et al., 40–62. Basingstoke: Palgrave Macmillian.

Aung San Suu Kyi, address given at the Methodist English High School Burma Reunion, 4th and 5th January 2013. Transcript from video tape.

Banerjee, A., and E. Duflo. 2011. *Poor economics: A radical rethinking of the way to fight global poverty.* New York: Public Affairs.

Beale Spencer, M., and C. Markstrom-Adams. 1990. Identity processes among racial and ethnic minority children in America. *Child Development* 61(2): 290–310.

Boonlue, W. 2012. Karen imaginary of suffering in relation to Burmese and Thai history. In *Present state of cultural heritages in Asia*, ed. S. Nakamura and Y. Yoshida, 21–26. Kanazawa: Kanazawa University.

Bourdieu, P., and J.C. Passeron. 1977. *Reproduction in education, society and culture.* London: Sage.

Boyden, J. 1993. *Families: Celebration and hope in a world of change.* London: Gaia and UNESCO.

Boyden, J. 2013. 'We're not going to suffer like this in the mud': Educational aspirations, social mobility and independent child migration among populations living in poverty. *Compare: A Journal of Comparative and International Education* 43(5): 580–600.

Boyden, J., and G. Crivello. 2014. Childwork and mobility. In *Migration: A compas anthology*, ed. B. Anderson and M. Keith, 37–38. Oxford: COMPAS.

Boyden, J., and J. de Berry. 2004. *Children and youth on the frontline: Ethnography, armed conflict and displacement*. New York: Berghahn.

Boyden, J., and J. Ennew. 1997. *Children in focus: A manual for participatory research with children*. Stockholm: Rädda Barnen.

British Sociological Association (BSA). 2002. Statement of ethical practice for the British sociological association. http://www.britsoc.co.uk/media/27107/StatementofEthicalPractice.pdf. Accessed 15 Nov 2015.

Buadaeng, K. 2008. Constructing and maintaining the Ta-la-ku community: The Karen along the Thai-Myanmar border. In *Imagining communities in Thailand: Ethnographic approaches*, ed. S. Takanabe, 83–106. Chiang Mai: Mekong Press.

Buckland, P. 2006. Post-conflict situation: Time for a reality check? *Forced Migration Review Supplement. Education and Conflict: Research, Policy and Practice*, July 2006: 7–8.

Camfield, L., G. Crivello, and M. Woodhead. 2009. Wellbeing research in developing countries: the role of qualitative methods. *Social Indicators Research* 90: 5–31.

Chakrabarty, D. 2000. *Provincializing Europe: Postcolonial thought and historical difference*. Princeton: Princeton University Press.

Chatty, D. 2010. *Displacement and dispossession in the modern Middle East*. Cambridge: Cambridge University Press.

Chatty, D., and G.L. Hundt (eds.). 2005. *Children of Palestine. Experiencing forced migration in the Middle East*. New York: Berghan Books.

Committee on the Rights of the Child (CRC). 2006. *General Comment No. 7, 2005*. Implementing child rights in early childhood. Geneva, 9–27 January 2006.

Cooper, E. 2014. Students, arson, and protest politics in Kenya: School fires as political action. *African Affairs* 113(453): 583–600.

Crisp, J. 2014. When you can't—Or don't want to—Go home again *Refugees International*. http://www.refintl.org/blog/when-you-cant-go-home-again#sthash.i7hLLA9s.dpuf. Accessed 17 July 2015.

Crisp, J., et al. 2001. *Learning for a future: Refugee education in developing countries*. Geneva: United Nations High Commissioner for Refugees.

Davie, G. 2007. *The sociology of religion*. Los Angeles: Sage Publications.

Demirdjian, L. 2012. Introduction: Education, refugees and asylum seekers—A global overview. In *Education, refugees and asylum seekers*, ed. L. Demirdjian, 1–37. London: Continuum.

Department for International Development. 2013. *Education position paper. Improving learning, expanding opportunities*. London: Department for International Development.

Falla, J. 1991. *True love and Bartholomew. Rebels on the Burmese border*. Cambridge: Cambridge University Press.

Fischer, T. 2014. Alt sein im ländlichen Raum. Zur Zukunft der häuslichen Betreuung und Pflege älterer Menschen. *Beziehungsweise. Informationsdienst des österreichischen Instituts für Familienforschung. Mai* 2014: 1–4.

Fischer, T. 2015. Unter einem Dach. Mehrgenerationenwohnen junger Frauen in steirischen Landgemeinden. *Beziehungsweise. Informationsdienst des österreichischen Instituts für Familienforschung. Jänner/Februar* 2015: 1–4.

Francis, Pope. 2015. *Laudato Si': On care of our common home.* Vatican City: CTS.

Ganjanapan, A. 1998. The politics of environment in northern Thailand: Ethnicity and highland development projects. In *Seeing forests for trees: Environment and environmentalism in Thailand*, ed. P. Hirsch, 202–222. Chiang Mai: Silkworm Books.

Gaonkar, D.P. 1999. On alternative modernities. *Public Culture* 11(1): 1–18.

Giddens, A., and P.W. Sutton. 2015. *Sociology.* Cambridge: Polity Press.

Goodman, R., and S. Harper. 2008. Introduction: Asia's position in the new global demography. In *Ageing in Asia*, ed. R. Goodman and S. Harper, 1–13. London: Routledge.

Gravers, M. 2012. Waiting for a righteous ruler: The Karen royal imaginery in Thailand and Burma. *Journal of Southeast Asian Studies* 43(2): 340–363.

Green, G., and E. Lockley. 2012. Communication Practices of the Karen in Sheffield: Seeking to Navigate their Three Zones of Displacement. *Asian Journal of Communication* 22(6): 566–583.

Gupta, A., and J. Ferguson. 2001. Culture, Power, Place: Ethnography at the End of an Era. In *Culture, Power, Place: Explorations in Critical Anthropology*, ed. Akhil Gupta and James Ferguson, 1–29. Durham: Duke University Press.

Harper, S. 2006. The challenge for families of demographic ageing. In *Families in ageing societies: A multi-disciplinary approach*, ed. S. Harper, 6–30. London: Routledge.

Harrell-Bond, B. 1999. The experience of refugees as recipients of aid. In *Refugees. Perspectives on the experience of forced migration*, ed. A. Ager, 136–168. London: Continuum.

Hart, J. 2004. Beyond struggle and aid: children's identities in a Palestinian refugee camp in Jordan. In *Children and youth on the front line: Ethnography, armed conflict and displacement*, ed. J. Boyden and J. de Berry, 167–186. New York: Berghahn.

Hart, J. 2008. *Business as usual? The global political economy of childhood poverty*, Young Lives Technical Note 13, Oxford: Young Lives.

Hart, J. 2014. Locating young refugees historically: Attending to age position in humanitarianism. *European Journal of Development Research* 26: 219–232.

Harvey, D. 2007. *A brief history of neoliberalism.* Oxford: Oxford University Press.

Hayami, Y. 2004. *Between hills and plains: Power and practice in socio-religious dynamics among the Karen.* Kyoto: Kyoto University Press and Trans Pacific Press.

Hendry, J., and S. Underdown. 2012. *Anthropology.* London: Oneworld Publications.

Hinton, P. 1983. Do the Karen really exist? In *Highlanders of Thailand*, ed. J. McKinnon and W. Bhruksasri, 155–168. Oxford: Oxford University Press.

Hondagneu-Sotelo, P., and E. Avila. 1997. I'm here but I'm there. The meanings of Latina transnational motherhood. *Gender & Society* 11(5): 548–571.

Huijsmans, R. 2013. 'Doing gendered age': Older mothers and migrant daughters negotiating care work in rural Lao PDR and Thailand. *Third World Quarterly* 34(10): 1896–1910.

Huijsmans, R.B.C., and T.T. Lan. 2015. Enacting nationalism through youthful mobilities? Youth, mobile phones and digital capitalism in a Lao-Vietnamese borderland. *Nations and Nationalisms* 21(2): 209–229.

Jeffrey, C., P. Jeffery, and R. Jeffery. 2008. *Degrees without freedom? Education, masculinities and unemployment in North India*. Stanford: Stanford University Press.

Jeffrey, C., and L. McDowell. 2004. Youth in comparative perspective: global change, local lives. *Youth & Society* 36: 131–142.

Kabeer, N. 2000. Inter-generational contracts, demographic transitions and the 'quantity-quality' tradeoff: Parents, children and investing in the future. *Journal of International Development* 12: 463–482.

Katz, C.F. 2004. *Growing up global: Economic restructuring and Children's everyday lives*. Minneapolis: University of Minnesota Press.

Keyes, C.F. 1977. *The golden peninsula. Culture and adaptation in mainland southeast Asia*. New York: Palgrave.

Keyes, C.F. 1991a. State schools in rural communities: Reflections on rural education and cultural change in southeast Asia. In *Reshaping local worlds: Formal education and cultural change in rural southeast Asia*, ed. C.F. Keyes, 1–13. New Haven: Yale Center for International and Area Studies.

Keyes, C.F. 1991b. The proposed world of the school: Thai villagers' entry into a bureaucratic state system. In *Reshaping local worlds: Formal education and cultural change in rural southeast Asia*, ed. C.F. Keyes, 89–130. New Haven: Yale Center for International and Area Studies.

Khan, H.T.A. 2013. Factors associated with intergenerational social support among older adults across the world. *Ageing International* 39: 289–326.

Knodel, J., et al. 2010. How left behind are rural parents of migrant children? Evidence from Thailand. *Ageing and Society* 30: 811–841.

Knodel, J. 2014. Is intergenerational solidarity really on the decline? Cautionary evidence from Thailand. *Asian Population Studies* 10(2): 176–194.

Kvale, S. 1996. *InterViews: An introduction to qualitative research interviewing*. Thousand Oaks: Sage.

Kyi, Aung San Suu. Address Given at the Methodist English High School Burma Reunion, 4th and 5th January 2013. Transcript from video tape.

Lareau, A. 1989. *Home advantage. Social class and parental intervention in elementary education*. London: Falmer.

Laungaramsri, P. 2001. *Redefining nature: Karen ecological knowledge and the challenge of the modern conservation paradigm*. Chennai: Earthworm Books.

Laungaramsri, P. 2003. Constructing marginality: The 'hill tribe' Karen and their shifting locations within Thai state and public perspectives. In *Living at the edge of Thai society: The Karen in the highlands of northern Thailand*, ed. C.O. Delang, 21–42. London: Routledge Curzon.

Laws, S., C. Harper, and R. Marcus. 2003. *Research for development: A practical guide*. London: Sage.

Levinson, B.A., D.E. Foley, and D.C. Holland (eds.). 1996. *The cultural production of the educated person: Critical ethnographies of schooling and local practice*. Albany: State University of New York Press.

Loo Shwe. 2015. Interview. 25 March 2015.

MacIntyre, A. 2002. Alasdair MacIntyre on education: In dialogue with Joseph Dunne. *Journal of Philosophy of Education* 36(1): 1–19.

MacLeod, J. 1987. *Ain't no makin' it. Levelled aspirations in a low-income neighbourhood*. London: Tavistock.

Hamer, Magali Chelpi-den, M. Fresia, and E. Lanoue. 2010. Éducation et conflits. Les enjeux de l'offre éducative ensituation de crise. *Autrepart* 2(54): 3–22.

Malinowski, B. 1922. *Argonauts of the western Pacific. An account of western enterprise and adventure in the archipelagoes of Melanesian New Guinea*. London: George Routledge & Sons.

Mann, G. 2004. Separated children: Care and support in context. In *Children and youth on the front line: Ethnography, armed conflict and displacement*, ed. J. Boyden and J. de Berry, 3–22. New York: Berghahn.

Mannheim, K. 1963. The problem of generations. *Psychoanalytic Review* 57(3): 378–404.

Maritain, J. 1943. *Education at the crossroads*. New Haven: Yale University Press.

Massey, D. 1994. *Space, place and gender*. Cambridge: Polity Press.

Mauss, M. 1990. *The gift. The form and reason for exchange in archaic societies*. London: Routledge.

Mayall, B., and V. Morrow. 2011. *You can help your country: English children's work during the second world war*. London: Institute of Education, University of London.

Metro, R. 2011. The divided discipline of Burma/Myanmar studies: Writing a dissertation during the 2010 election. *Cornell Southeast Asia Program Bulletin* 2011: 8–13.

Metro, R. 2013. Postconflict history curricula revision as an 'intergroup encounter' promoting interethnic reconciliation among burmese migrants and refugees in Thailand. *Comparative Education Review* 57(1): 145–168.

Moore, J. 2014. Protection against the forced return of war refugees. An interdisciplinary consensus on humanitarian *non-refoulement*. In *Refuge from inhumanity?: War refugees and international humanitarian law*, ed. D.J. Cantor and J.-F. Durieux. Laiden: Stanford University Libraries.

Myint Swe, J. 2014. *The cannon soldiers of Burma*. Toronto: We Make Books.

Newman, S., and A. Hatton-Yeo. 2008. Intergenerational learning and the contributions of older people. *Ageing Horizons* 8: 31–39.

Ong, A. 2006. *Flexible citizenship. The cultural logics of transnationality*. Durham: Duke University Press.

Pells, K., and M. Woodhead. 2014. *Changing children's lives: Risks and opportunities*. Oxford: Young Lives.

Phan, B. 2015. Interview, 10 April 2015.

Phan, Z. 2009. *Little daughter. A memoir of survival in burma and the west*. London: Pocket Books.

Platz, R. 2003. Buddhism and Christianity in competition? Religious and ethnic identity in Karen communities of northern Thailand. *Journal of Southeast Asian Studies* 34(3): 473–490.

Puaschunder, J.M. 2014. *The call for global responsible intergenerational leadership in the corporate world: The quest of an integration of intergenerational equity in contemporary corporate social responsibility (CSR) models*. New York: The New School, Department of Economics.

Rajah, A. 1990. Ethnicity, nationalism, and the nation-state: The Karen in Burma and Thailand. In *Ethnic groups across national boundaries in mainland southeast Asia*, ed. G. Wijeyewardene, 102–133. Singapore: Institute of Southeast Asian Studies.

Renard, R.D. 1980. *Kariang: History of Karen-Thai relations from the beginning to 1923*. Ph.D. diss., University of Hawaii.

Robinson, B. 2015. Interview, 13 March 2015.

Rogers, B. 2004. *A land without evil. Stopping the genocide of Burma's Karen people*. Oxford: Monarch Books.

Rogers, B. 2012. *Burma. A nation at the crossroads*. London: Ryder Books.

Rogoff, B. 2003. *The cultural nature of human development*. Oxford: Oxford University Press.

Sadan, M. 2003. Textile contexts in Kachin state. In *Textiles from Burma. Featuring the James Henry Green Collection*, ed. Elizabeth Dell and Sandra Dudley, 169–177. London: Philip Wilson Publishers.

Saunders, B., J. Kitzinger, and C. Kitzinger. 2015. Anonymising interview data: Challenges and compromise in practice. *Qualitative Research* 15(5): 616–632.

Schröder-Butterfill, E. 2005. The impact of kinship networks on Old-Age vulnerability in Indonesia. *Annales de démographie historique* 2: 139–163.

Scott, J.C. 2009. *The art of not being governed. An anarchist history of upland southeast Asia*. New Haven: Yale University Press.

Shwe, Loo. 2015. Interview, 25 March 2015.

Skinner, D., and D. Holland. 1996. Schools and cultural production of the educated person in a Nepalese hill community. In *The cultural production of the educated person: Critical ethnographies of schooling and local practice*, ed. B.A. Levinson, D.E. Foley, and D.C. Holland, 273–299. Albany: State University of New York Press.

Somé, M.T.A. 2012. Familles en survie dans un espace défavorisé à Ouagadougou. In *Negotiating the livelihoods of children and youth in Africa's urban spaces*, ed. M.F.C. Bourdillon, 33–48. Dakar: Council for the Development of Social Science Research in Africa.

Spradley, J. 1980. *Participant observation*. Fort Worth: Harcourt Brace College Publishers.

Stein, E. 1989. *On the problem of empathy*. Washington, D.C.: ICS Publications.

Stern, T. 1968. Ariya and the golden book: A millenarian sect among the Karen. *The Journal of Asian Studies* 27(2): 297–328.

Stone, L. 1994. Modern to postmodern: Social construction, dissonance, and education. *Studies in Philosophy and Education* 13: 49–63.

Tan, Y.S., and R. Santhiram. 2014. *Educational issues in multiethnic Malaysia*. Petaling Jaya: SIRD.

Thang, L.L. 2015. Creating an intergenerational contact zone: Encounters in public spaces within Singapore's public housing neighbourhoods. In *Intergenerational space*, ed. R.M. Vanderbeck and N. Worth, 17–32. London: Routledge.

Thang, L.L., and M.S. Kaplan. 2013. Intergenerational pathways for building relational spaces and places. In *Environmental gerontology: Making meaningful places in old age*, ed. G.D. Rowles and M. Bernard, 225–251. New York City: Spring Publishing Company.

Thawnghmung, A.M. 2008. *The Karen revolution in Burma: Diverse voices, uncertain ends*. Washington, D.C.: East-West Center.

The Border Consortium. 2014. *The Border Consortium. Program Report July–December 2014.*

Toyota, M. 2005. Subjects of the nation without citizenship: The case of 'hill tribes' in Thailand. In *Multiculturalism in Asia*, ed. B. He and W. Kymlicka, 110–135. Oxford: Oxford University Press.

Turner, D. 2015. *The old boys. The decline and rise of the public school*. New Haven: Yale University Press.

United Nations. 2015. *The millennium development goals report 2015*. New York: United Nations.

UNESCO (United Nations Educational Scientific and Cultural Organization). 2010. *Reaching the marginalized*. Education for All Global Monitoring Report 2010. Oxford: Oxford University Press.

UNESCO. 2015. *Education for all 2000–2015: Achievements and challenges*. Paris: UNESCO.

UNHCR. 2014a. *Kayin state profile*. UNHCR South-East Myanmar Information Management Unit.

UNHCR. 2014b. *UNHCR projected global resettlement needs*. 20th Annual Tripartite Consultations on Resettlement Geneva: 24–26 June 2014.

Vaddhanaphuti, C. 1991. Social and ideological reproduction in rural Northern Thai schools. In *Reshaping local worlds: Rural education and cultural change in southeast Asia*, ed. C.F. Keyes, 153–173. New Haven: Yale University Southeast Asia Studies.

Vanderbeck, R.M. 2007. Intergenerational geographies: Age relations, segregation and re-engagements. *Geography Compass* 1(2): 200–222.

van der Geest, S. 2002. Respect and reciprocity: Care of elderly people in rural Ghana. *Journal of Cross-Cultural Gerontology* 17: 3–31.

van Hear, N. 2009. The rise of refugee diasporas. *Current History* 108(717): 180–185.

van Vliet, W. 2011. Intergenerational cities: A framework for policies and programs. *Journal of Intergenerational Relationships* 9(4): 348–365.

Vaughan, M., and M.S. Archer. 1971. *Social conflict and educational change in England and France, 1789-1848*. Cambridge: Cambridge University Press.

Vogler, P., G. Crivello and M. Woodhead. 2008. *Early childhood transitions research: A review of concepts, theory, and practice*. Working Papers in Early Childhood Development 48, The Netherlands: Bernard van Leer Foundation.

Wagner, D.A. (ed.). 2015. *Learning and education in developing countries: Research and policy for the post-2015 UN development goals*. New York: Palgrave.

Walker, A. 2001. The 'Karen consensus', ethnic politics and resource-use legitimacy in Northern Thailand. *Asian Ethnicity* 2(2): 145–162.

Watson, K. 1994. Caught between Scylla and Charybdis: Linguistic and educational dilemmas facing policy-makers in pluralistic societies. *International Journal of Educational Development* 14(3): 321–337.

Weber, M. 2002. *The protestant ethic and the 'spirit' of capitalism and other writing*. London: Penguin.

Weber, M. 2013. Ethnic groups. In *Economy and society. An outline of interpretive sociology*, ed. G. Roth and C. Wittich, 385–398. Berkeley: University of California Press.

Whitehead, A., I.M. Hashim, and V. Iversen. 2007. *Child-migration, child agency and inter-generational relations in Africa and South Asia*. Brighton: Development Research Centre on Migration, Globalisation and Poverty.

Williams, C.H. 1996. Ethnic identity and language issues in development. In *Ethnicity and development: Geographical perspectives*, ed. D. Dwyer and D. Drakakis-Smith, 45–85. Chichester: Wiley.

Willis, P.E. 1980. *Learning to labour. How working class kids get working class jobs*. Aldershot: Grower Publishing Company Limited.

Winichakul, T. 1994. *Siam mapped: A history of the geo-body of a nation*. Chiang Mai: Silkworm Books.

Yousafzai, M. 2013. *I am Malala. The girl who stood up for education and was shot by the Taliban*. London: Phoenix.

CHAPTER 2

Sociocultural Learning and Work in the Family

Sociocultural learning has always been important and continues to be the centre of education in increasingly complex societies in a globalized world (Boyden 1993). Learning differs according to historical times and geographical places. For example, at the end of the seventeenth century, the philosopher John Locke promoted a curriculum that recommended the acquisition of practical tasks:

> for a Country-Gentleman, I should propose one, or rather both these: viz. Gardening or Husbandry in general, and working in Wood, as a Carpenter, Joyner, or Turner, these being fit and healthy Recreations for a Man of Study, or Business. For since the Mind endures not to be constantly employ'd in the same Thing, or Way; and sedentary or studious Men, should have some Exercise, that at the same time might divert their Minds, and employ their Bodies: I know none that could do it better for a Country-Gentleman, than these two, the one of them affording him Exercise, when the Weather or Season keeps him from the other. Besides, that by being skill'd in the one of them, he will be able to govern and teach his Gardener (Locke 1699: 363).

Locke was thus favourable for a balanced education that trained the whole person through intellectual and practical activities so as to enable the country gentleman to become an adult capable of directing and helping his gardeners. Similarly, John Dewey observed that prior to the spread of schooling 'there was continual training of observation, of ingenuity, constructive imagination, of logical thought, and of the sense of reality

P. Jolliffe, *Learning, Migration and Intergenerational Relations*,
DOI 10.1057/978-1-137-57218-9_2

acquired through first-hand contact with activities' (Dewey 1974: 298). Dewey (1974) worried that in complex societies the need for formal and intentional learning increases to such an extent that there would be a danger of creating an undesirable split between experiences gained through direct learning and what is acquired at school. Accordingly, he suggested transporting the teaching of practical tasks from the domestic and community level to institutional school settings. In this respect, he saw particular value in 'helping others' (Dewey 1974: 298). Indeed sociocultural learning can foster intergenerational relations. Typically, elders introduce younger ones gradually to the mastery of skills that allow them to assume increasing responsibility for managing situations and particular tasks. In this way, through their practical activities, boys and girls contribute as active agents to the transformation of cultural tools, practices and institutions that shape the historical and dynamic nature of community life (Rogoff 2003: 89). Among the Karen sociocultural learning continues to be important within families and communities. A senior is typically perceived as older, stronger and more experienced, which in turn implies a superior social status. A junior is seen to be younger, weaker, less experienced and of lower status. Typical examples of senior-junior relations are parents and children, teachers and students, richer and poorer households. Importantly, these relations are reciprocal and entail social obligations and benefits for both parties. The junior pays respect and obedience to the senior, while the senior, in turn, returns these respectful signs through benevolent acts, hence supporting the welfare of juniors. Senior-junior relations permeate all levels of society, ranging from the intimacy of the household to national and international politics (Vogler 2010). As economies change, so do senior-junior relationships.

Work in the Family

Among the Karen people in Burma and Thailand, intergenerational learning takes place from early childhood as children assist adults with simple chores in the household economy. In the past, sociocultural learning was not perceived as a form of education. For example, regarding the Karen in Burma, the missionary Paolo Manna wrote at the beginning of the twentieth century:

> Of what does the education consist that the parents give their children? (...) [T]ere is neither the word nor the idea of education. (...) It is all reduced to material care, similar to what the hen has for her chicks. When a child is

two or three years old, he is left to his own devices. If it's a girl, then she has something to do; she should take care for her younger brother or sisters when the mother is not in the house. These poor little girls learn very quickly how to become little mothers. When they are six or seven years old, they begin to lighten the mother's tasks. If the mother goes to draw water or to get some wood, the little girl follows her with her tiny little basket, and happily carries her portion of the burden (Manna, quoted in Emmons 1964: 67–68).

This quotation highlights the sentimental writing style of early twentieth century missionaries. For example, expressions like 'these poor little girls' could nowadays be misinterpreted as patronizing. Today we also know that work during childhood is neither morally dubious, nor harmful. Instead, it forms part of their cultural learning at home and at school. Children learn through watching, listening and practice. Shared working activities are important for liaising and therefore confirm intergenerational relationships. Contemporary theories of sociocultural learning, too, emphasize the importance of practical skill acquisition during childhood and youth transitions. Work inspired by Vygotskyian sociocultural psychology emphasizes childhood development as a universal maturational process which differs in content according to local ethno-theories. For example, Barbara Rogoff's concept of 'guided participation' draws attention to both the active engagement of children in their social world as well as the role of adults and peers in guiding children towards full participation in culturally valued activities. Although the process of guided participation is universal, it differs according to the degree of communication between children and their caregivers, as well as in the skills expected from mature community members in a given cultural and historical context (Rogoff 2003: 285–287).

Also among the Karen, traditional forms of learning and education are embedded within the context of everyday life of their communities. During fieldwork in 2008 and 2009 I observed how Karen children come to be familiar with the gendered social roles of adults from an early age. Boys and girls mostly 'played' until around the age of five. The play of young children often consisted of imitating adult behaviour through observation and practice. Toddlers accompanied others in the rice field and play alongside their working families. Boys also 'played' catching birds, imitating the hunting activities of their older peers. Mothers asked toddlers to go with them to take care of the buffalo or just stay around while they prepare food with an older sibling: thus children learned through watchful participation in the cultural routine of cooking.

Until the age of five, children helped with washing dishes and fetching water. Then, around the age of seven, children's contribution to household chores increased gradually. Girls spent much more time in the household than boys. They started earlier in life to help their elders with household tasks such as fetching water, cooking rice, washing dishes and clothes and cleaning. They also knew how to wash themselves and their own clothes. Some girls cared for younger siblings, for example by taking them along when playing with their peers. Boys worked less inside the household than girls. They contributed to providing for the household, for example, through watching and herding the family cattle, fishing with spears, as well as hunting snakes or birds with slingshots. Boys were aware of the privilege of being able to move around, and often value it highly. At the age of ten or so, children were considered to have achieved their first responsibilities. For example, instead of just cooking the rice, girls were by that age entrusted with the preparation of side dishes. This way, adults conveyed to children the idea of contributing little bits to the successful completion of larger working processes. With the onset of their teenage years, working responsibilities increased. At this age, they could also be sent to work with other families to help them with their household chores. By the age of twelve, girls and boys were fairly familiar with the gendered mastery of culturally valued tools and technologies. Weaving was still a traditionally female activity, whilst boys learned to work with the plough and hunting tools such as slingshots and guns. Most girls learned weaving from their grandmothers, mothers, other female relatives or foster mothers.

Sometimes, girls produced a garment together with a more experienced weaver. In general, girls are considered more mature than boys. At the age of 12, boys and girls also participated in unpaid seasonal agricultural work on villager's fields. The hot and rainy seasons were the most labour-intensive periods for rice production and children's working assistance was highly demanded. School holidays covered cultivation and harvesting periods, hence allowing children to fully support their household's subsistence economies. Rural development processes also impacted on young peoples' transition to adulthood. Among the Karen, at the time of fieldwork, a youth became an adult when he was economically independent. As outlined above, in a subsistence economy, children reached the status of economic independence of adults by the age of 12. This age usually coincided with mastery of culturally relevant working skills, such as weaving and ploughing. In an expanding market economy, rising educational aspirations and growing household need for cash, young peoples' adult status is linked with their ability to earn an income. At the time of writing this book, children's financial contributions to the household income were increasingly important. My study found children around the age of 15 assuming responsibility for income generation at different occupations. Therefore, processes of uneven development in rural mountainous areas of northern Thailand impact on patterns of intergenerational working activities among the Karen.

Intergenerational Relations and Rural Development

As societies change, so do ideas about parents' and children's proper roles. According to Dewey, in more complex societies the gap between the capacities of children and the standards of adult behaviour increases. He believed that education alone can bridge this generation gap (Dewey 1966: 2–3). He also observed that prior to the spread of schooling 'there was continual training of observation, of ingenuity, constructive imagination, of logical thought, and of the sense of reality acquired through first-hand contact with activities' (Dewey 1974: 298). Dewey worried that in complex societies the need for formal and intentional learning increases to such an extent that there would be a danger of creating an undesirable split between experiences gained through direct learning and what is acquired at school.

At the fieldwork site in Chiang Mai, commercialized agriculture was introduced in 1976 through a Royal Agricultural Project. Since then, intergenerational working activities in the family have changed. For instance, because of the scheduled working hours at the Royal Project women in Huay Tong find it difficult to prepare food in the evening. Very often, this task is handed over and becomes the responsibility of teenage daughters. Moreover, with most adults working at the Royal Project, hunting and gathering tasks have been delegated to boys and girls. This gave way to the emergence of new intergenerational responsibilities children have towards their parents. Most households relied on the help of teenagers to earn cash income. Karen teenagers were aware of the economic value of their work as contributions to household economies. They usually combined their studies with income generation for their households. Assisting their parents added value and meaning to their work and made them feel good: 'I like it, because I can help mother, and she does not have to feel tired. I feel well when I can help mother, it makes me be someone who is not lazy'. Like this, during the time of fieldwork most high school girls in the village found paid employment with the Royal Project during weekends and school holidays. Especially during labour-intensive periods, such as the rainy season, intergenerational solidarity was important and mothers asked daughters to cover their working hours at the Royal Project. That way, the mothers were free to transplant rice in their own fields. Moreover, commercialized agriculture at the Royal Agricultural Project was also perceived as a 'safe haven' for unemployed youth. Somchai's life course drawing illustrates this (Fig. 2.1).

In 2008 Somchai was 16 years old and had just graduated from lower secondary school. At that time, he said he would like to move to the lowlands and learn to be a mechanic. In addition he said he would be interested in studying agriculture academically in order to become a researcher in this domain. He said that during his studies he would stay a while outside the village. However, he expected to be unemployed when he was 30. After losing his job, Somchai explained he would return to Huay Tong for unpaid work. For example, in his drawing (Fig. 2.1) he portrayed himself at 35 roaming the forest as a hunter equipped with a gun. This indicates he knows how to earn a livelihood in the forest. At the age of 40, he antici-

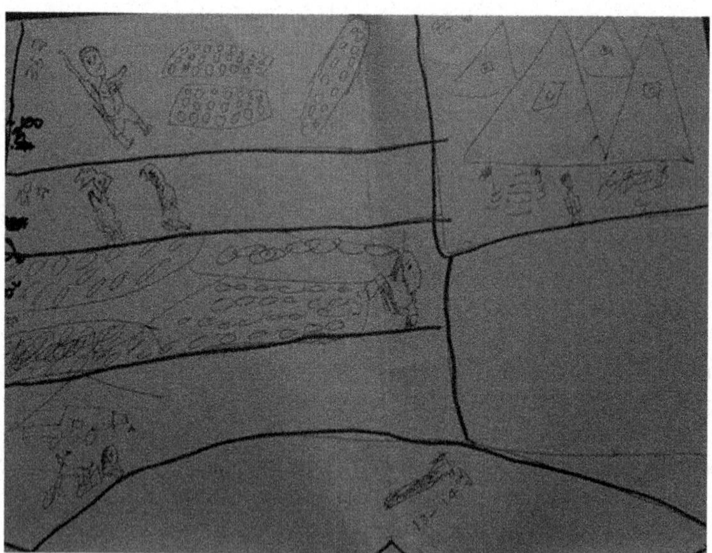

Fig. 2.1 Somchai's life course drawing, June 2008

pated being employed at the Royal Agricultural Project. When I revisited the village in December 2013, Somchai's twin sister said he was working in a hotel in Chiang Mai. He occasionally sends money to support their mother who suffers from HIV/AIDS. So, intergenerational solidarity and interdependence between girls' and boys' work and their family and village economies are very important in young peoples' life ambitions.

Social Morality and Children's Working Activities

I have outlined gendered, generational and socio-economic diversity among children's working activities earlier. This section turns to the ethical and cultural values underlying young peoples' work. I explain how the work of boys and girls relates to local work ethics of labour exchange and interdependence as well as more globalized labour ideologies—such as the value of economic thrift—pertaining to industrialization and global political economy. Research on the changing values of young people's time use highlights how the moral distinction of childhood from adulthood emerged in nineteenth-century Western Europe. At this time, social discourses started speaking of children's 'misuse' of time and expressed concern about the moral risks of 'idleness'. In *The Children of the Poor*, Cunningham (1991) demonstrates how ongoing redefinitions of 'idleness' problematized the activities of socially marginalized children, thus creating a dominant idea of 'proper childhood'. Indeed 'idleness' was believed to enhance the propensity to crime. Street children were portrayed as on the verge of mischief and described as 'savages', 'tribes of lawless freebooters' and even animals (Cunningham 1991: 128).

In Thailand, relations between adults and children are relations of reciprocity. Work during childhood is neither considered morally suspicious nor harmful. At the time of conducting this research, the work of girls and boys formed part of their cultural learning at home and at school. Parents valued their children's contribution to the household. The importance of children's working contributions is succinctly expressed in the Karen saying that 'you have to pay back the milk you drink from your mother'. Most parts of young people's work was not considered work (*ngaan*) but assistance (*chuai*). This implies that there is someone else with overall responsibility for the outcome of the task. On the one hand, this means that the assisting person cannot be blamed for potentially negative results, but on the other hand he or she does not receive full recognition for successes or accomplishments. Furthermore, the expression *chuai gan* (to assist each other) implies equality amongst all those involved in the working process. One situation of *chuai gan* is, for instance, when a school asks parents to help with major, though non-remunerated tasks, on the school compound such as tearing down old buildings and rebuilding new ones. Also, if teachers help each other, they are considered *chuai gan*. Children's assistance in adult work is '*chuai*' (to assist), since the overall responsibility of the task rests with the leading adult and is not distributed equally as in *chuai gan*. During fieldwork I observed boys and girls assisting their seniors both in the village and at school. In these processes, collaboration of peers is necessary for completing tasks in the village and at school. Having their company makes activities enjoyable and valuable in the children's eyes: 'It is fun, because I go with friends'. Therefore, in the eyes of local adults and children, economic activities are important for socializing with peers and seniors and therefore confirm mutual bonds and friendships.

Diligence and Laziness

Assisting seniors through unpaid work, therefore, offered the opportunity to demonstrate diligence and an overall good character. Assisting others through unpaid or paid work allowed girls and boys to show that they are diligent. Diligence, in turn, is highly valued among Thai and Karen people. In exchange for their services, children may gain the benevolent support of a teacher, a senior relative or a priest. Support through intergenerational relationships turned very important, for example, for planning of school transitions. Karen youth of lower status, such as foster children, enhance their social position through unpaid work and good behaviour. Through their diligent work assisting at school, boys and girls secure the benevolence of local mediators like Thai teachers who help them access scholarships for higher studies. The value of assisting or helping others was further revealed in children's gendered life course aspirations. For example, the occupations of nurse and policewomen were related to the virtue of helpfulness: 'I want to be a policewoman because I like to help others'. Diligence is also a major criterion for determining whether someone is overall 'a good girl' or 'a good boy'. Karen and Thai students described a 'good girl' or a 'good boy' as someone who is not lazy, who studies, who speaks well, who does not walk around and does not travel by night, who thinks well, and who has a smiling face all the time so that others around are happy. In contrast, a bad girl or boy is selfish, unhelpful, smokes cigarettes and drinks alcohol. At the time of writing this book, Karen society expected girls, in particular, to demonstrate modest and industrious behaviour: '(Y)oung Karen women should be quiet, tidy and primarily take care of domestic work. Any young women talking too much and going out of their home very often will be seen as behaving improperly as women' (Naiyana 2001: 104). Good girls 'help their parents, go to church' whereas not-so-good girls are 'escaping school and don't like to listen to their parents'. Through diligent behaviour, children avoided being regarded as 'lazy'. For instance, a 16-year-old girl explained that assisting her mother made her feel 'unlazy'. Throughout fieldwork it transpired that 'lazy' and 'diligent' do not always refer to the performance of girls and boys in all domains of life. Rather, these values inform whether a person meets the expectations of a senior like a parent or teacher in a particular social context. Children and adults can be perceived as 'lazy' in one domain like intellectual activities and at the same time as 'diligent' in another such as work. For example, in 2008 at Huay Tong school in Chiang Mai province, Deif was not a particularly dedicated student. He had already repeated one year and had little ambitions to study further. However, at the same time, he was also very active in helping with all kinds of mending work on the school compound. Moreover, he was well known as a talented entertainer and often contributed at school performances, singing songs to teachers' high-ranking guests such as the school inspector. Because of his comic talent, he was also very popular among his peers at school and functioned even as student representative during his last year at Huay Tong school. Because of all his extracurricular activities everyone at school considered Deif as talented and diligent, his low grades notwithstanding. The examples of the two boys Sanya and Hpa Sav Hsoof also illustrates the flexibility of the notion of 'lazy'. After graduation from Huay Tong school, Sanya and Hpa Sav Hsoof enrolled for higher education at the Agricultural Polytechnic College in Sanpathong. They only stayed for a few months before deciding to leave. In an interview in 2008, Sanya explained his decision: 'Because at that time I like to study more than work. In Agricultural College there is more work than study, you are farming, go and walk plant beans. I am not lazy to work. But at that time I was not yet adult. I wanted to study' (Sanya Kasetsukchai, interview, 28 May 2008). By contrast, Hpa Sav Hsoof returned to Huay Tong. However, in the eyes of his sister Naw Hpe Nay: 'he was lazy and returned. But, he liked to work' (Naw Hpe Nay, 8 June 2009). So, Hpa Sav Hsoof was thought of as 'lazy to study' because he wanted to work. By contrast, Sanya had to avoid being labelled as someone 'lazy to work' because of his aspirations for more formal education than what was offered at the Agricultural Polytechnic College. In both cases, 'laziness' seems to indicate personal value dissonance with the expectations and ideas of others, such as households or village communities.

Household Interdependencies

As outlined above, Karen girls' and boys' economic activities ideally fit into a wider sociopolitical context of family and community life. Accordingly, their life ambitions are interdependent with the economic needs of their families and communities.

The occupational aspirations of primary school boys and girls reflect the values and needs of their households. In 2008, Div Hsei, an 11-year-old boy in Huay Tong, said that after graduation from Huay Tong school he wanted 'to go and learn becoming a mechanic' and re-enrol in vocational studies alongside this. Afterwards, he planned to return to Huay Tong because 'I am happy with my family. I want to stay with my parents'. He envisaged opening a garage and 'if there is any money' to give it to his parents. His peer Pit had different aspirations as he wanted to study for a bachelor's degree. Nevertheless he also emphasized that he wanted to 'get a job to assist my family'. Teenage boys and girls also valued their work when they saw that it related to their household and therefore helped them be 'good'. They were aware of the importance for their work to contribute to their household economies. In Ban Kad, 11 students told me that the best thing about work was the possibility to earn extra money to support their parents and to contribute to their study expenses. Nine persons said they liked their work because they could help their relatives with income generation and eight said it was because they could find good learning experiences for life through this work.

Arguably, the value of a job decreases the more they feel it is 'tiresome'. A girl from Nong Tau village engaged in seasonal agricultural work on lowland farms during weekends and applied for jobs with the local administration during school breaks: 'If you ask about "likes" there are things I like and dislike because the work that I do there are some parts that are tiring and others which are not. But if I can choose, I rather do a better job that is more comfortable and not hard and which also allows me supporting my parents'. Others felt that their work was tiresome, but the social, moral or financial advantages outweighed the negatives and rendered the job worthwhile. For instance, students appreciated engaging in 'honest work' even if it was tiring. Another classmate helped her uncle grill pork liver for 130 baht per day. She used the money for her studies and for gasoline. She said about her working activities: 'sometimes I like it, sometimes not, sometimes I am frustrated and tired with it, but I have to persevere. If I don't persevere there is no money'. Boys and girls who become a financial drain to their households are not thought of well. Occasionally, I heard stories of teenage boys who dropped out of school because they struggled to finish their higher education in the lowlands. Often, they left school and searched for employment without informing their households. So they continued for a while to receive money from their parents for studies while also generating their own income. They are said to be prone to mischief. A young Karen woman described them as: 'naughty. They do not really study, they go and find employment in the city'. Moreover, in the eyes of Karen householders, youth employment loses its value when it challenges generational power relations within the household and/or the socio-economic status of the household vis-à-vis others. Problems arise when the working activities of young men and women are coupled with a strong aspiration for independence and transition to full adulthood. Adults may even try to curb male teenagers' aspirations for earning money when this income goes towards private expenses, such as alcohol consumption or gasoline. For instance, in February 2008 I observed a clash between three young men and their foster mother Maliwan. It was the peak season for picking strawberries. Like many other adults, over one weekend, the three boys took the opportunity to earn 100 baht a day by helping with the strawberry harvest. They travelled to the workplace with a peer who owned a motorcycle. Upon their return on Sunday evening, the foster parents reproached them for their behaviour and inquired why they felt the need to earn money if everything is free in their house, including clothing, housing and food. The boys argued that they needed the money to 'play somewhere'. In this case, the foster father suggested, the youth should also contribute to the household with their salary. Thus confronted with the full implications of adult responsibility, the young men agreed not to work for cash anymore. Preventing youth from paid working activities also speaks about socio-economic status. Not all parents can afford to withdraw their sons from the formal labour market. In Huay Tong, I heard parents of higher socio-economic status commenting that they prefer their teenage sons to help them with their own rice cultivation than work elsewhere for money. For example, although there existed the possibility for income generation at Sanpathong Agricultural Polytechnic College, the mother of Fee preferred her son to return during weekends to help her with rice cultivation for their household: 'it is better to help the mother than to be employed'. Interdependencies between young peoples' work and their household economies is therefore very important when it comes to the social morality of children's economic activities.

Children's Occupational Aspirations

My data suggest that Karen boys and girls are aiming for attractive, middle-class careers within wider Thai society. In participatory research exercises children's representations of such occupations are slightly gendered. They emphasize their need for institutional intermediaries in achieving their occupational goals. My data also reveal teenagers' awareness of the labour market's structural limitations. Girls and boys know they cannot rely blindly on the supportive structures of modern institutions. In addition, household economies may suddenly require young people's working presence. Thus, boys and girls negotiate their individual job aspirations against the reality of an insecure labour market and household interdependencies.

Individual case studies highlight how the context (whether political, economic, social or cultural), shapes young peoples' intergenerational relationships and aspirations in different households and places.

For example, Fee's life course drawing clearly illustrates intergenerational relationships during working activities in his past childhood and his future adult life (Fig. 2.2).

According to his life course drawing, in 2008 Fee expected to finish his studies and learn the skills of a mechanic in the lowlands. Afterwards, he planned to return to Huay Tong and to work for the Royal Agricultural Project. At the same time, he wanted to continue working with his parents, hence contributing to the household income. Furthermore, he said he would like to earn an academic doctorate and afterwards cultivate his own vegetables and keep cows as well as chickens. He emphasized he wanted to have two cars and a house. The idea of two cars indicates an aspiration towards upward social mobility because his family owned one already. Therefore they were considered as one of the economically better-off villagers. When I revisited Huay Tong in 2013, his mother told me Fee was continuing his studies outside the village and visited the family regularly.

Tik also planned to migrate for education and work out of her village (Fig. 2.3).

According to her drawing, in 2008 Tik planned on leaving the village temporarily for studies and to work in town. She envisaged a school tran-

Fig. 2.2 Fee's life course drawing, June 2008

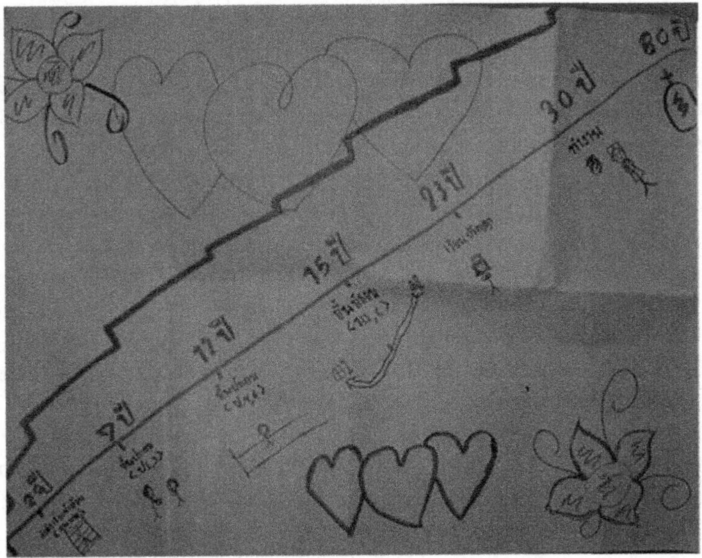

Fig. 2.3 Tik's life course drawing, May 2008

sition to secondary school in Chang Dao district. After graduation from high school she considered continuing her studies at a nursing school in the city. At the age of 30 she thought she would work as a nurse. Tik also expressed her wish to return to Huay Tong, where she said she would like to live her adult life. Finally, Tik also revealed in her drawing that she hoped to make her final transition—from life on earth to life eternal—in Huay Tong and be buried in her home village. When revisiting Huay Tong in December 2013 I met Tik who had just returned to her village for Christmas with her family. We saw each other during Christmas celebrations in the village and this was when she told me she was attending 11th grade at a higher secondary school in Ban Kad—a different school than the one she thought she would attend back in 2008.

The case studies of Naw Eu and her friend Naw Mugi also illustrate how life courses may develop in different ways. I met Eu during fieldwork in 2008. She was the second of three siblings in a Buddhist-Christian household in Huay Tong. Her parents cultivated their own garden and rice field.

Eu's family earned additional income thanks to Eu's mother's employment with the Royal Agricultural Project and some production of alcohol for sale in the village. Since I met Eu in 2008 her working and learning activities were connected to the needs of her family. Intergenerational relations are particularly strong between Eu and her mother, a Catholic Christian married to a Buddhist man. Like her mother, Eu is a Catholic and participates in Buddhist ceremonies when visiting members of her father's side of the family. Since childhood Eu's working activities have been interdependent with her home and related to the wider national economy. For example as a teenager, in order to help her mother, Eu took on a lot of economic responsibilities. At home, she was responsible for preparing food. She downplayed her own cooking talents, saying that she only made rice. However, once we became friends, she invited me for evening meals and I learned that she was also in charge of preparing side dishes, a skill usually reserved for mature women in a Karen household. This highlighted to me her ability to take decisions.

Eu's economic activities were also linked to the wider regional and national economy. During weekends, she helped with income generation at the Royal Agricultural Project. She replaced her mother, for example, in working with saplings in a greenhouse. This allowed her mother to cultivate their family garden. During school holidays, Eu accompanied her mother for half-day work in their garden. Eu's mother valued her daughter's working activities. As a recognition of her solidarity and also as a sign of confidence, Eu's mother granted her certain freedoms other girls her age did not enjoy. For example, Eu was allowed to use the family's mobile phone. Access to the telephone enhanced her social status among her peers. Eu used the mobile phone to build up social relations with her peers, for example lending the phone to her girlfriends, who otherwise had no way to make or receive calls. At Huay Tong school, Nau Eu was a good student and very responsible. After graduating from Huay Tong lower secondary school, Eu made the transition to a high school in Mae Sot (Tak Province) in May 2009. In this way, she left her native village Huay Tong and moved as a foster child into the household of her older maternal uncle in Mae Sot. This uncle was a widower with two adopted Karen children from Burma. One of the children was a handicapped girl on crutches. Since she and Eu were the same age, Eu was called to help in the household and befriend the girl. As a foster child, Eu did the laundry, cooked rice and side dishes and drove her peers on the motorbike to school. Because of the geographic distance between Mae Wang and Tak province, it was impossible for Eu to return to her home village regularly, except for major seasonal school holidays.

In 2008, Eu and her friend Mugi took part in participatory research exercises. Together they prepared a drawing of a life course line that tells about their ambitions for adult life, including becoming air hostesses (Fig. 2.4).

When I met Eu again between November 2013 and January 2014 she was enrolled in a teacher training programme at the Buddhist Wat Chedi Luang in Chiang Mai. Her ongoing formation has been made possible through a church-based scholarship programme run by the Jesuit Order in Chiang Mai. Eu was specializing in Thai language with the aim to teach the Thai national language as a school subject in primary and lower secondary schools and she told me that with this formation she would hope to find employment in the highlands and help Karen children to learn Thai. As in the past, Eu still had a very good relationship with her mother and tried to visit her home village every weekend. During these visits, she assisted her parents with household tasks and income generation at the Royal Agricultural Project. In late 2013, Eu was 21. She told me she was not yet thinking about marriage and childbearing because she wanted to finish her studies first. By contrast, her friend Naw Mugi married a man from Mae Hong Son in December 2013. She was already five months pregnant. Mugi and her husband usually worked in Chiang Mai as car-

Fig. 2.4 Eu and Mugi's life course drawing, June 2008

ers for elderly people. They also support relatives in the Karen villages in the highlands. Their wedding was in the mountains because according to Karen tradition a wedding takes place in the bride's home village, followed by a ritual visit to the groom's native village. So compared to their aspirations in 2008, both Eu's and Mugi's lives turned out differently than planned. While both emigrated to receive secondary education to different places, none of them became an air hostess. Instead, in 2013 Mugi married and prepared for motherhood, while Eu continued to be enrolled in tertiary education in order to become a teacher of the national language and assist younger generations with Thai.

My research evidences how families aspire for their children's secondary and if possible even tertiary education and children emigrate to different locations and institutions of learning. Despite this general trend of emigration, my research suggests that young people maintain a sense of intergenerational solidarity. While employment situations in cities and towns are unstable, intergenerational relations are safety nets which allow young people to aspire to return to their native villages for marriage and childbearing and to support their household and village economies through paid and unpaid economic activities.

Bibliography

Boyden, J. 1993. *Families: Celebration and hope in a world of change.* London: Gaia and UNESCO.

Cunningham, H. 1991. *The Children of the poor: Representations of childhood since the seventeenth century.* Oxford: Blackwell.

Dewey, J. 1966. *Democracy and education. An introduction to the philosophy of education.* New York: The Free Press and Collier-Macmillian Limited.

Dewey, J. 1974. The school and society. In *John Dewey on Education.* Chicago: The University of Chicago Press. 297–306.

Emmons, C.F. 1964. *The Ghekhu by Paolo Manna, Translated and Annotated.* Thesis, Urbana. Illinois.

Kasetsukchai, Sanja. 2008. Interview, 28 May 2008.

Locke, J. 1699. *Some thoughts concerning education.* London: Black Swann.

Naiyana, V. 2001. *The transformation of gender roles in resource management of a Karen community in Northern Thailand.* Master Thesis, Chiang Mai University.

Naw Hpe Nay. 2009. Interview, 8 June 2009.

Rogoff, B. 2003. *The cultural nature of human development.* Oxford: Oxford University Press.

Sanja Kasetsukchai. 2008. Interview, 28 May 2008.

Vogler, P. 2010. *Translocal identities. An ethnographic account of the political economy of childhood transitions in northern Thailand.* DPhil, University of Oxford.

CHAPTER 3

The Value of Schooling

Schools have played an important role in nation building around the world. In the global political economy, throughout the world children spend increasing amounts of time in modern schools. Research on the changing values of young people's time use highlights how the moral distinction of childhood from adulthood emerged in nineteenth-century Western Europe. Before that children learnt by means of work and apprenticeship (Ariès 1996: 186–187). Until the sixteenth century, boys typically spent two or three years in school studying Latin, the language of commerce, administration and religious affairs (Turner 2015: 3). In the UK the term 'public school' refers to the large ancient private schools, like Eton. Girls' public schools usually focused on music, dancing and needlework. Training in Latin, Greek, French and arithmetic seemed unimportant, even for girls of high social status (Turner 2015: 52). And yet, Queen Elizabeth I received a comprehensive classical education and was taught foreign languages as early as the sixteenth century, a time when the idea that a woman should be silent and subservient was widely promoted and accepted. Elizabeth's education is particularly interesting because people never thought she would be queen and therefore she was not being educated for this role. Possibly her tutors recognized her phenomenal brain from a young age and encouraged and developed it. Although William Grindal was her official tutor, the princess also received through Catherine (Kate) Champernowne, Roger Ascham, John Cheke, Robert Cox and

P. Jolliffe, *Learning, Migration and Intergenerational Relations*,
DOI 10.1057/978-1-137-57218-9_3

Jacques Belmain a thorough grounding in Latin and Greek as well as in French and Italian. By her 12th birthday everyone who met the princess was impressed by her intellectual and womanly accomplishments (Loades 2006: 55).

Thus, social status and gender largely determined what kind of education children received. For instance, John Locke wrote in his treaty *Some thoughts on education* (1699): 'Each Man's Mind has some peculiarity, as well as his Face, that distinguishes him from all others: and there are possibly scarce two Children, who can be conducted by exactly the same method. Besides that I think a Prince, a Nobleman, and an ordinary Gentleman´s Son should have different ways of Breeding' (Locke 1699: 379–380). This diversity among children has largely been ignored by other Enlightenment philosophers, like Jean-Jacques Rousseau who promoted rather sentimental and homogeneous ideas of childhood development. In his famous treaty *Emile, ou l'education* Rousseau established a linkage between nature, childhood and education. For Rousseau, learning begins right at the beginning of life: 'our education begins with our birth; and our first teacher is our nurse' (Rousseau 1893: 9). Discussions about education and the proper role of youth and children marked this period. In *The Children of the Poor* Cunningham (1991) demonstrates how ongoing redefinitions of 'idleness' problematized the activities of socially marginalized children, thus creating a dominant idea of 'proper childhood'. Unoccupied or 'idle' children were perceived as a threat to society and potentially capable of undermining state authority. It is noteworthy that 'idleness' here refers to children outside institutional structures such as households or the labour market, who gained their livelihood either through begging in urban spaces or vagrancy in the countryside. Moreover, 'idleness' was believed to enhance the propensity to crime. Street children were portrayed as on the verge of mischief and described as 'savages', 'tribes of lawless freebooters' and even animals (Cunningham 1991: 128). Similarly, Roman Catholic missionaries perceived Karen children in Burma as wild and close to nature. In 1902, Paolo Manna wrote comparing Karen children with Christian children in Italy:

> I see the children of these people growing up like so many animals, dirty, always naked, playing in and getting covered with dust and dung, and I think of our children raised in cotton clothes among the cares and solicitudes of very loving mothers (...) The boy becomes an adolescent, then a man, and in everything he has always done as he has pleased, has followed

> his whim, free with the savage freedom of the beasts of the wood. If the boy doesn´t want to go to school, why would the parents ever oppose him? (Manna, quoted in Emmons 1964: 69)

In this quotation we can perceive the unease with regard to children who are growing up outside institutional structures like nursery or school. The missionary worried about children's hygiene and about boys turning into strongly willed young 'with the savage freedom of the beasts of the wood.' Manna noted that this freedom, coupled with a strong will, was even capable of opposing parents' encouragement of school. His attitude reflects a general European tendency that from the late nineteenth century perceived the work and freedom of children as a hazard, and school as the only place where children should spend their childhood (Cunningham 1991: 90; Zelizer 1985). Based on Rousseau's ideas, mission schools were built all over the British Empire, starting with infant schools for very young children (May et al. 2014: 5–7). In Burma and Thailand, schools run by missionaries started to introduce Western education to the Karen from the seventeenth century.

Missionary Schools in Burma

In Burma, for several centuries, children's access to formal education was largely determined by gender, religion and social status. Formal education was largely provided by Buddhist monasteries. In pre-colonial Burma almost every village had a Buddhist temple school 'where all the boys of the village learned the alphabet and the elements of their religion and all of them, rich and poor alike, shared in the menial duties of the establishment' (Furnivall 1957: 29–35). Some boys migrated from surrounding villages and stayed in dormitories within the temple compound. They usually learnt how to read and write the ancient language of Pali, Buddhist philosophy and sometimes even medicine.

From the sixteenth century onwards, Catholic missionaries visited the kingdoms of Ava and Pegu, often in the company of Portuguese merchants and mercenaries (Myint Swe 2014: 271). The status of these Westerners was unsettled. They migrated from town to town and also got caught up in internal political conflicts that lead to the execution of famous personages such as Filipe de Brito who was captured during the 1613 conquest of Syriam (Socarras 1966: 6).

Diplomatic relations between East and West improved in the seventeenth century when the East India Company opened up trade in Siam and Burma (Sangermano 1893: xxii–xxiii). In 1719, Pope Clement XI sent a group of Barnabite priests (Clerics Regular of St Paul) to China. In 1721 these priests sent a missionary—Father Calchi—to the kingdom of Pegu, where King Taninganwe understood the value of European knowledge and technology. He even encouraged the immigration of Italian missionary teachers for the education of young people at the Royal Court. In a letter to his superiors, Father Calchi wrote that the King 'desires other missionaries and men expert in the arts of painting and weaving cloths, making glass, astronomers, mechanics, geographers etc., to instruct his subjects in the way of the spirit and make them more cultivated in human sciences, of which they are most capable' (Calchi 1723, quoted in Ba 1964: 290–291) Of course, the Italian missionaries had to prepare themselves by learning the local languages Mon and Burmese. Mastery of these official languages, in turn, enabled them to compile grammars and dictionaries of these languages. Over the years they asked their brethren in Italy to send kind teachers and abundant supplies of teaching material such as books; sacred and profane pictures, and architectural designs for churches and buildings; paintings, geographical maps and books for church music. With these items the missionaries planned to teach a curriculum that included subjects such as geometry, astronomy, mathematics, as well as practical skills such as carpentry, building fountains and compounding medicines, as well as cooking, distilling perfumes and making cakes 'because everything is precious and new here' (Calchi 1723, quoted in Ba 1964: 290–291). Diplomatic relations between the Holy See and Burma became very close in the reign of King Mindon who held foreign visitors in high esteem and bestowed the Catholic priests, like the Armenian priests and Chinese monks, with tokens of kindness. The Royal Family even valued the education of girls. In 1863, the crown prince entrusted Bishop Bigandet with four little girls to be placed in the care of nuns in a convent in Rangoon. There, the girls were to be educated as European girls of their age were. The prince paid for their boarding and sent occasional presents until his assassination in 1866. After his tragic assassination, the King himself continued to pay for the girls' education for a period of two years. Afterwards, three of them obeyed the King's orders to return to Mandalay whereas one girl decided to stay with the nuns in the convent (Bigandet 1887: 75). Thus, early missionaries were called to the Burmese Royal Court to instruct boys and girls close to the Royal Family. In this way, mutual trust was built and the missionaries obtained Royal permission to open schools for poorer children in other parts of the country.

The Italian missionaries were accustomed to ministering to a multi-cultural and multi-ethnic congregation and therefore turned into important intermediaries between local people, such as the Karen and other foreigners, including the British ambassador Michael Symes who noted the Karens' distinctive socio-economic and cultural life. In *An Account of the Kingdom of Ava* (1800), Michael Symes described the Karen in the following way:

> They lead quite a quiet life and are the most industrious subjects of the state (…) They profess and strictly observe universal peace, not engaging in war or taking contests for dominion, a system that necessarily places them in a state of subjection to the ruling power of the day. Agriculture, the care of cattle, and rearing poultry, are almost their only occupations. A great part of the provisions used in the country is raised by the Carianers, and they particularly excel in gardening (Symes 1800: 207).

The ambassador had received this information from the Italian missionary Vincentius Sangermano, who 'seemed a very respectable and intelligent man, spoke and wrote the Birman language fluently, and was held in high estimation by the natives for his exemplary life and inoffensive manners' (Symes 1800: 206). Sangermano had a clear understanding of the lives and livelihoods of the Karen as well as their marginalization because of their preference of peace over contestations for political power. Upon his return to Italy, Sangermano composed a description of the laws and customs of the peoples of Burma. This text remains an important historical source.

Not all missionaries shared Sangermano's sensibility for Karen culture. For instance, at the beginning of the twentieth century, Paolo Manna complained about the lack of hygiene and wrote: 'the filthiness of these people is really a test for the missionary no matter how strong a stomach he has' (Manna, quoted in Emmons 1964: 29) Schooling, Manna and his predecessors hoped would change the morality and manners of the Karen.

Among the Poor

The first Western teacher training school was built with royal permission by the Barnabite missionaries in Syriam. Although the school was destroyed during the war between Ava and Pegu, it was rebuilt after the arrival of

Father Nerini in Syriam in 1749. It was the first school built of bricks and cement according to European school architecture. The school educated a group of Burmese youth according to the principles and guidelines of the Barnabite Colleges in Italy. Father Nerini also built a church next to the school and two boarder houses, one for boys and one for girls. The students came from different ethnic backgrounds, such as Burmese, Peguans, Armenians and Portuguese. This school was not only teaching reading and writing but also geography, arithmetic and nautical sciences. Imitating the pattern of Barnabite high schools in Europe, the school was self-sufficient thanks to the attached farms and workshops, poultry pens and pigeon cotes (Ba 1964: 295). Father Nerini was also known for his enthusiasm for the culture and customs of the peoples of Burma. He revised a grammar and dictionary of the Burmese language. In addition, he compiled a catechism and prayer book. He also knew the Karen and visited them frequently: 'the zeal of Nerini took him among some savage populations who lived separate from others in full liberty, and are called Karens (Cariani)' (Sangermano 1893: 283).

Itinerant missionary teachers continued to instruct local children. In 1761, Father Maria Percoto from the Missionary Congregation of Saint Paul arrived in Burma to support the Barnabites. Soon after his arrival several priests died. Therefore, Percoto found himself faced with the challenge of a whole range of practical requirements of missionary work, including teaching and travelling to different locations, including to the Karen of whom he wrote: 'The Karen are also a savage tribe in this region. They use another language full of monosyllables which they pronounce gargling in the throat, and with a mumble and an unpleasant whistle' (Percoto, quoted in Griffini 1781: 123). In the absence of other priests and teachers, Percoto started to travel with a group of local students through the country side. He described his migratory teaching experience:

> Seeing myself all alone to look after the Christians, I am forced to be continually on tour. My family is made up of one hundred and fifty men and boys, the greater part of whom depend entirely on me… some are paying students, and some have been confided to me by their parents to that I may bring them up in the religion and in letters…My children help me in everything. Some as catechists, some as interpreters in important matters; some help me in the management of the school and the functions of the church; according to their ages some teach the others: I superintend everything and provide for all. (Letter dated 11 February 1766, quoted in Ba 1964: 298)

This migration of teacher and pupils continued for a period of five years until another batch of missionaries arrived and started building schools at missionary stations. Percoto himself hoped to develop an already existing Barnabite school and seminary building. However, the local Buddhist monks claimed ownership over the land. As a result, the Italian priests—with the help of a French infantryman at the court—had to pull down the building and reconstruct it at another site (Griffini 1781: 155–159). This incident shows that notwithstanding royal permission to open schools, social tensions accompanied the building of Western institutions of learning. Indeed in his official records, Bishop Bigandet noted how many attempts at starting a mission among the Karen in Pegu failed in spite of permissions granted by ministers and provincial governors. Major obstacles were persons who circulated false reports about the intentions and activities of the missionaries (Bigandet 1887: 42–43).

Despite these local disputes and contestations, the missionary school system expanded. Students either lived in the same village or migrated from surrounding areas to the school compound. The schools were usually managed by local masters or mistresses. With these schools, Bishop Bigandet hoped to reform the local education system which was based on rote learning: 'They learn by heart sometimes an astonishing number of words, but the teacher never takes the trouble to explain anything to show the relations between one idea and another, to lead the lad to draw an inference. The knowledge they acquire is purely mechanical instead of being a well prepared food for the intellect. In fact, the capabilities, nay the very existence of the mind is practically ignored by the pretend teachers of youth' (Bigandet 1887: 63). As we shall see in Chaps. 5 and 6, rote learning and confrontational teaching with little student participation continue to characterize predominant patterns of learning in schools in Burma and Thailand.

In 1840, the Oblate missionaries started their education work with the Karen boys near the port town Bassein, located in the province of Pegu. This community was quite international and multi-ethnic. Since the sixteenth century, descendants of the Portuguese merchants and mercenaries have been living in Bassein. In this way a small Christian community developed throughout the seventeenth century. Again, in the eighteenth century, European merchants and Armenians settled in the port town. The community was furthermore composed of a number of Karens living in the neighbourhood. To attend to the spiritual needs of this international

Christian community, a Barnabite missionary priest used to visit them at least once a year (Bigandet 1887: 96–97).

In 1860, the construction of another Bassein school started. The work was put under the direct supervision of a French missionary, Father Dumollard, who was assisted by a group of 12–15 Karen youth. At the time of its completion, the school was called St Peter's Institution. The school counted 62 students from Bassein and a similar number of boarder students who migrated from surrounding villages for education at St Peter's. At this school, Karen boys learned how to read and write in English and Burmese. In addition, the students—almost all Karen boys—were trained in several handicrafts, including photography, carpentry and smithery. The purpose of the school was the development of Karen and Burmese according to the rules of European schools. This is how the Bishop hoped to train an adult generation of craftsman, teachers and catechists. Very talented boys and girls even made the transition to a College in Penang where they studied Latin. In the surroundings of the school, a small noviciate was built. In addition, a printing press was installed next to the school building. For the use of letter press printing, the community received types, i.e. pieces of metal with raised letters or characters on its upper surface. So as to write in the English alphabet, the community types from French missionaries in Calcutta donated the types for printing the alphabet and the Burmese types came from the Baptist Mission Press which was founded in 1816 in Rangoon (Howard 1931: 38). In this way the missionaries printed a prayer book in Burmese and school books for the teaching of the alphabet, geography, arithmetic and religion (Bigandet 1887: 99). An English day school for girls was built close to St Peter's School, together with an orphanage and a Burmese school for the daughters of Karen Christians who dwelt in villages around Bassein. The teaching and management were entrusted to two Burmese nuns who arrived from Rangoon and Bishop Brigandet prayed that 'under God's blessing it is to be hoped that the Institution will prove productive of much good for the benefit of the Karen population' (Bigandet 1887: 100).

Girls' schools started all over the country. The French missionary Father Bringaud started building his girls' and boys' schools outside the village of Oukpho in 1874. The girls' school was a two-storey building made of teak with enough space for two mistresses and a number of boarder girls. The female teachers were native nuns of the congregation of St Francis Xavier. These girls typically stayed on the school compound because of the great distance that separated them from the villages where their parents lived. The school compound was enclosed. In its garden there were plantains, mango and tamarind trees and the children learnt how to recognize suitable grounds to cultivate flowers and a few European vegetables (Bigandet 1887: 108).

In 1876, two more schools—one for Karen girls and one for Karen boys—were built in Mayoka (Maryland). The girls' building was made out of brick. In spite of these new building materials, working conditions in rural schools remained harsh. Usually, missionaries adapted to the Karen lifestyle. In Mayoka, the priest in charge lived in a bamboo hut and four to five families began to dwell around this hut. His food was described as being of 'the coarsest description hardly better than that of the poor Karen' (Bigandet 1887: 101–102).

The American Baptists

At the beginning of the nineteenth century, American Baptist missionaries arrived in Burma. Those famous American Baptist missionaries are Adoniram Judson, Jonathan Wade and George Dana Boardman. During the three Anglo-Burmese wars in the years 1826, 1852 and 1886 Burma was gradually incorporated into the British Empire. Throughout the colonial period, the British always administered the people in the hills separately from the rest of Burma. This time affected the Karen relationship with the British profoundly. The Karen became close to Baptist missions and British officials. The American Baptist educational activities were influential in forming the first ideas of a 'Karen' national identity. This led to the emergence of a Christian-led Karen ethno nationalism in Burma.

The first Baptist missionary who is said to have met the Karen was Adoniram Judson, the son of a Congregationalist minister. In 1812, he and his wife, Anne, went as missionaries to India. There, they met British Baptists, left the Congregationalists and joined the American Baptists. As such they went from India to Burma where they actively engaged in missionary work. Judson studied Burmese and soon embarked on translating the Bible into this language whilst his wife, Anne, learned Siamese (Thai) and translated the gospel of Matthew. As mentioned above, the Bible had already been translated by the Catholic missionaries. Judson seems to have recognized these translations but found them overall 'too Romish' (Howard 1931: 30) so he decided to translate the Bible again from scratch. Jonathan Wade (1798–1872) and his wife Deborah Wade (1801–1868) also settled in Moulmein, learnt Burmese and Sgaw Karen. Wade built a church and a school in 1828 and his wife taught in a school, but without a fixed schedule, since the demands of the moment had priority over adherence to fixed schedules: 'She did much personal hand-to-hand work in leading the women to Christ'. Indeed it was common practice for individual Karen teachers to send selected Karen students for English language instruction and Bible study to the home of missionaries (George Dana Boardman, quot. in King 1835: 169). During one of these home visits, a Karen man called Ko Tha Byu, discovered in the house of Adoniram Judson the Book of Common Prayer and wondered whether this might be the legendary lost book his ancestors had told him about. He converted and after his baptism in 1828 subsequently visited many Karen villages announcing the return of the 'white brother' and of the 'gold book'. This news, in turn, is said to have caused the conversion of hundreds of Karen (Marshall 1997: 296). John Wade's biographer also notes that a group of Karen asked Wade 'Teacher give us the Karen books'. Jonathan Wade learnt how the Karen believed they used to have access to the written language but had lost it. According to their ancestral legend, foreigners were meant to bring it back again. This episode is said to have caused Jonathan Wade to undertake the work of putting the Sgaw Karen language into writing (Wyeth 1891: 79–80). Therefore, Scripture was by some Karen understood as the 'lost book' and this offering of literature, together with health and the message of salvation, had a strong impact on the Karen. Because of the legend the missionaries thought the hearts of the Karen were well prepared to welcome the sacred book of the Bible: 'the prophecy of the return of the white brother with the Lost Book, which inspired the Karen with the hope of a better future and furnished an admirable foundation on which Christian teachers could build in promoting the development of the Karen nation' (Howard 1931: 58).

Formal theological training among the Karen began in 1836 in Tavoy and in 1845 a Karen theological school was built in Moulmein and later moved to Rangoon. Moulmein was in the early days the centre of education. From 1871 onwards American women societies' sent women missionaries to Moulmein. Consequently, until 1900, 39 high schools and scores of primary schools were established. The famous Judson College began in 1872 as Rangoon College. The College was at first a middle and high school, until 1920, when with the addition of a bachelor's degree, it became Judson College and a constituent part of the University of Rangoon (Hall Hunt 2005: 350). Because many students were Karen, it was nicknamed 'Karen College' and became a centre for the development of Karen nationalistic ideas.

The large-scale establishment of missionary schools was important for the formation of a growing sense of Karen-ness within and beyond local communities. During the nineteenth and twentieth centuries, many literate Karen assumed roles within and between different village communities. In 1880 the Burma Baptist Convention sent three Karen missionaries to Thailand, where they established a church in the Chiang Mai province (Rogers 2004: 53–54). One year later, in 1881, Christian Karen founded the Karen National Association, a forerunner of the Karen National Union. The principal aim of the Association was the promotion of Karen identity, leadership, education and writing, independent of members' religious belief (Smith 1999: 44–45). This emergent Karen nationalism was particularly promoted by those Karen who were allied with the British after their conquest of lower Burma, central Burma and upper Burma. Especially during the Second World War, the Karen joined the British against the Burmese. This provided the ground for the future ethnic conflict between the Karen and the Burmese in Burma (Keyes 2003: 213).

After the student protests in 1988, universities in Burma essentially shut down and a whole generation of students lost the opportunity to enrol in higher education (Hall Hunt 2005: 352). Therefore, compared to the past, today few Karen graduate from secondary school in Burma. Those who graduate are often unable to speak sufficient Burmese to communicate well with authorities and to make the transition to the national tertiary education system (Lall and South 2014). Limited access to tertiary education, in turn, means that minority groups have less chance to participate in the already ongoing education reforms and curricula revisions at both sides of the Thailand-Burma border (Metro 2013).

Catholic Schools in Thailand

For centuries education in Thailand had been linked to religious institutions. Buddhist temples provided boys with the opportunity to study and work as novices. During the reign of Ayutthaya's King Phra Narai Maharaj, at the end of the seventeenth century, French Catholic missionaries were granted permission to open schools. Apart from religious teaching, the curriculum included modern subjects and the King allowed members of the Royal family to study there. Yet upon the death of King Narai in 1688, the missionaries lost royal protection. As a consequence they closed schools and left the country (Wyatt 1969). A secular Western education system was only introduced under the reign of King Rama IV, in the second half of the nineteenth century. At this time Siam was working on its own process of nation building and required people with a modern education to work as bureaucrats in the new institutions. Because of the expanding activities of British Burma and Indochina, Siamese authorities felt the need to engage with British and French colonial powers and to participate in their legal system of treaties and bureaucratic language. In 1887 the Department of Education was established. In 1898, the Royal Thai government introduced a law ordering a nationwide system of education based on modern curricula. Schools were graded into primary, secondary, occupational and higher education categories. In 1909 the running of schools was removed from the Buddhist Sangha, but in the absence of well-trained secular teachers, monks continued teaching in government schools until the mid-1930s. Throughout the 1920s many monks actively participated in promoting the new school system, for example, through sponsoring fundraising activities on local temple grounds. The nationalism promoted by King Rama VI declared the Buddhist religion, Thai Royalty and the Thai nation as the three pillars of national identity. Sangha authorities remained supportive of state schools, not least because Buddhist moral instruction was included in the curriculum (Keyes 1991: 96–100). The proclamation of the Compulsory Education Act in 1921 obliged all children between the ages of 7 and 14 to attend schools with centralized curricula and Central Thai as the language of instruction. For the first time in Thai history, education was made available on a large scale for boys and girls. Once more, Christian missionaries were granted permission to build schools in Thailand. Public Catholic schools became particularly popular among the urban Thai Buddhist elite who aspired to Western education for their children. In 1924 the Ursuline Sisters of the Roman Union arrived in Thailand. The Sisters work focused on education. In 1928 they started teaching classes at the newly built Mater Dei ('Mother of God') School in Bangkok. Although the school was for girls, boys were admitted to the kindergarten and first two grades of elementary school. In Chiang Mai, the Regina Coeli School was opened in 1932. This school, too, was a primary and secondary school for girls. In the same year, the Brothers of St. Gabriel opened Montfort School for boys in Chiang Mai (Montfort College 2015: #School history; Roman Union of the Order of St Ursula, Thailand 2013:# A brief history). There was also the Sacred Heart School offering co-education for girls and boys. This school was opened by The Society of Foreign Missions of Paris (Société des Missions étrangères de Paris, M.E.P.).

The curricula of these schools mirrored the demand for international languages. For example, at Mater Dei School, children learnt Thai and English during primary school. From secondary onwards, they also studied French. Following the transition from an absolute monarchy to a parliamentary system and liberalism in 1932, even more emphasis was laid on the development of a centralized education system. Accordingly, in 1936 Mater Dei School in Bangkok changed its curriculum to conform with the curriculum of the Thai Ministry of Education.

In general, Catholic schools were open to children of different faiths: for example, in 1962 only 40 students in all the Catholic educational institutions in Thailand were Catholics (Gomane 1964: 11). Graduates from these schools made the transition to Chiang Mai University where they enrolled in Humanities, Social Sciences and Sciences. The majority of these students were ethnic Thai. Buddhist and Christian schools in the cities attracted children from high social classes. At the same time, Buddhist and Christian missionaries started to reach out to marginalized populations. In this way from the 1950s onwards increasing numbers of Karen started accessing primary and secondary education in the highlands of northern Thailand. Indeed the Catholic Church has been a key engine in promoting formal education long before the expansion of state-sponsored schools. Buddhist missionaries, too, targeted Karen youth through educational programmes. In 1965 the Phra Dhammacharik ('Wandering Dharma') Programme, a Buddhist missionary project, was initiated in the mountains. The explicit purpose of the project was religious education and the development of future monks. Similar to priests, missionary monks helped to link Karen boys with temple schools in the lowland plains where they were ordained as novices and received an education. Boys increasingly took up this educational opportunity and became ordained as novices in large city monasteries, such as Wat Srisoda in Chiang Mai city. After finishing secondary school in the city wat, some boys were selected to become missionary monks and sent on missions to highland villages. Today, Wat Srisoda in Chiang Mai continues to attract hundreds of boys from poor regions (Hayami 2004: 205; Buadaeng 2003: 251).

Therefore, until the late 1970s, highland children mostly accessed formal education through the structure of religious networks. They relied on Christian and Buddhist missionaries for information and transportation. Priests and monks acted as cultural intermediaries between the highlands and lowlands. Through their mediation, Karen students started attending formal schooling at city temples and at Thai government as well as private Christian learning institutions.

The emergence of Christian-led Karen nationalism in Burma discussed earlier barely influenced the Karen in Thailand. Although there were occasional exchanges of pastors and priests (Rogers 2004: 52–54), these exchanges were curbed in the wake of the Second World War, when education in Thailand was linked to Thai nationalism. The Karen were largely excluded from dominant ideas of Thai-ness. Thus marginalized, the Karen in Thailand continued to live according to their ancestral ways in their local environments without significant participation in modern schools (Keyes 2003: 214).

However, this changed in the 1950s when in the wake of the Cold War Thai authorities watched with apprehension the growing civil strife in Burma and the expansion of Communism in China as well as in the border region between Thailand and Burma. At this time a wave of Christian missionaries was forced to leave China and settled in Thailand. It was in this way that the Fathers of the Bétharram Congregation arrived in Thailand.

In an attempt to counter communism, the Royal Thai government endorsed Christian missionaries' activities among ethnic minorities in the highlands (Buadaeng 2003: 214; Hayami 2004: 47). Once the Royal Thai government gave permission to open a school, it also contributed with monthly financial aid towards the running of the missionary school. School management was usually in the hands of missionary priests and the aid usually depended on the number of students and was used for the general maintenance of the school building as well as the daily school lunches. Father Carlo Luzzi from the Bétharram congregation recalls in an interview: 'They gave us financial aid. How should we otherwise have been able to entertain all these people? Because at noon, the students did not leave school. There was a refectory and personnel to prepare a meal. And the students were also happy' (Luzzi, interview, 26 March 2015).

In addition, government prescribed the uniforms for girls and boys. Parents had to cover the costs for these uniforms and also for the stationery used at school. In addition, there were always a number of students who received aid from the missionaries. The rules and regulations of the school were the same as in government schools and the medium of instruction was Thai. The students spoke their native mother tongue outside school. In Chiang Rai, for example, Father Luzzi taught children from primary school up to high school. The exams were the same as the official government exams in Thailand. Therefore, the government personnel were very happy with Christian missionary schools. Students who wanted to continue their education went to a state high school or a public school like Montfort or Regina Coeli in Chiang Mai. Some students even went on to study medicine at University and the authorities employed students who had been to missionary schools. Therefore, authorities saw these missionary schools in a favourable light and recognized that they provided developmental aid to the country. Father Luzzi compares this process with scaffolding: the mission helped the government to expand schooling in the country side. Luzzi, who taught for 15 years in Chiang Rai, felt that the Thai authorities appreciated the missionary schools (Luzzi, interview, 26 March 2015).

Mae Pon School

In the highlands of rural northern Thailand, the Catholic Mae Pon School and Buddhist Wat Srisoda were the first free schools accessible to Karen boys and girls. In 1955, priests of the French Bétharram Congregation founded the Mae Pon School. Father Joseph Seguinotte, in particular, became known as the founding father of the school. Throughout the 1950s, the school was an innovation in the hills of northern Thailand. Indeed before the establishment of Mae Pon, there was no formal education available for Karen children who were non-Buddhists in the highlands of northern Thailand. Even among Buddhist children, it was only boys who received free education in Buddhist monasteries, whilst girls remained at home. Mae Pon was the first school open for girls and boys with different religious backgrounds. Although Mae Pon School was not an official government school, Thai authorities supported and appreciated the educational project of the Bétharram missionaries (Luzzi, interview, 26 March 2015). During his life time Father Seguinotte himself compiled the first edition of a Karen dictionary to Thai, English and French languages. The handwritten manuscript of 1,500 pages was eventually edited and published by the Jesuit Father Alfonso de Juan, SJ (de Juan 2007: xi–xii). Compared with government schools, Mae Pon did not require children to wear uniforms. Instead, they were allowed to wear their homespun Karen dresses. Children were also free to choose their hairstyles, whereas at government schools there is a prescribed hairstyle for girls and boys at different school levels. In spite of these differences, children at Mae Pon always learned Thai civic behaviour such as paying respect to the Thai King through the flag-raising ceremony and singing of the national anthem at morning assemblies, a practice shared by government schools all over Thailand. Thai was also taught at school, whereas the medium of instruction was Karen. In 1970, a former female graduate of Mae Pon initiated, with Father Seguinotte, an agricultural project where students at Mae Pon learned about the theory and practice of agriculture. The initiative came from a young Karen adult woman who after a period of migration for education returned to the mountains to help her people. After completion of her secondary school she had moved to Chiang Mai where she attended an agricultural college for two years. Through the agricultural project at Mae Pon she wanted to apply the knowledge and skills acquired at the school. This is a good example of intergenerational transmission of knowledge and experience (*Feuilles Missionnaires* 1970: 10).

From the moment of the school's inception, Karen children migrated from all over Chiang Mai to Mae Pon School. In an interview, Chumpol Maniratanavongsiri recalled that from 1957 onwards children from Huay Tong village started migrating for education to Mae Pon. Earlier none of them went to school, and education consisted only of sociocultural learning as described in Chap. 1. The distance between the village in Mae Wang and Mae Pon School was significant; it required children to travel on foot for two days through the jungle. Usually, a group of twenty children walked, in the company of two or three adults. Because of the distance, children only returned to their home village during school breaks. The school season started in June and lasted until October. This was followed by a break before studies were resumed from January to April. So, the school breaks coincided with labour-intensive periods when children were expected to support their household economies with rice cultivation (Maniratanavongsiri, interview, 11 February 2008). For example, in an interview Prasert Trakansuphakon, also known by his Karen name Pav Di, remembered returning to his village during the school break. During this time he dedicated himself entirely to work with his family. In this way, intergenerational relations were strengthened and maintained. It would have been awkward had he not been able to do any practical work for his household and community: 'we felt hunger to know what young people know in the village and to do the work they do'. Indeed in addition to Mae Pon School, the family and the village continued to be important locations of learning. In Karen society, boys are generally close to their fathers. When the women go to work in the rice fields, men go hunting. So, from the age of five onwards, Pav Di went with other boys into the forest to hunt birds and rats with stones and bows. At around the age of 12 he was allowed to accompany other men for hunting with gun and gunpowder. Pav Di recalled perfectly well the first time he used his father's gun to shoot a squirrel. He was standing on a stone in the middle of a stream using the gun which ricocheted with such a force that it fell into the water and left him with a pain in his shoulder. However, when he returned to the village his uncle, the younger brother of his father, was very proud of him and asked what he had hunted. When he saw the squirrel he commented 'oh, your father will love it!' Pav Di also remembers his mother being very proud, because he was like the father. There were also days of collective hunting. Once, when he was 15, Pav Di went with two elder male relatives, his brother-in-law and father, to hunt a barking deer (Trakansuphakon, interview, 15 July 2008). These memories highlight the ongoing importance of intergenerational relations and sociocultural learning in the lives of the Karen people even when they go to school. Pav Di confirms that receiving mother-tongue-based education at the Catholic Mae Pon school enabled him to be proud of his Karen cultural heritage, because his teachers were Karen. Teachers frequently told children to be proud of their Karen culture and use their education to help their communities (Trakansuphakon, email, 9 July 2015). Therefore, Pav Di was keen on learning both informal and formal skills and knowledge at home and at school. In this way he incorporated being initiated into the traditional skills of hunting while he successfully attended the missionary school in Mae Pon and later made the transition to Montfort College in Chiang Mai. Over the years, Mae Pon School developed a curriculum for Karen children who, in addition to attending the obligatory Thai government school, wanted to learn the Karen language. Children's learning outcomes confirmed UNESCO findings with regard to the benefits of mother-tongue-based education from early childhood on. According to this research, learning and the developing literacy skill in their mother tongue does not prevent children from acquiring proficiency in a second language (Ball 2011: 27). Indeed at Mae Pon children started to learn in their Karen mother tongue and then continued with the learning of Thai and English. Because of the sound formation in children's mother tongue, the children learned easier and faster a second or even third language. For example, Pav Di remembers his transition from Mae Pon School to Montfort College in Chiang Mai. During his first examination in grade 4 in Montfort College he reached top scores in English language. His teachers and classmates were surprised, because in their view Pav Di had just arrived from the forest school of Mae Pon. Pav Di himself believes that it was the mother-tongue-based multilingual learning process at Mae Pon school that enabled him to secure very good results (Prasert Trakansuphakon, email, 9 July 2015).

Educational Pathways

Missionary schools in Thailand opened up new educational pathways for Karen children. During ongoing fieldwork with the Karen in northern Thailand it transpired that leading Karen intellectuals and professionals in non-governmental organizations, universities and religious institutions had attended these schools. Whilst in the past agriculture as part of the village subsistence economy was the only professional activity Karen boys and girls were educated towards, schooling introduced them to new and various ways of income generation. This holds particularly true for girls and children with disabilities; while these children would have been extremely marginalized in a traditional skill-based subsistence economy, schooling developed their intellectual capacities and prepared them for participating in Karen society. For example, the teacher Kru Tip Suksawad, also known by his Karen name is S'raf Peilei, was one of the first Karen boys with physical disability to attend Mae Pon School. He subsequently attended a seminary and became a teacher. First he worked as a religious teacher and was later appointed as a teacher with the Public Welfare Department. In 1967 Kru Tip arrived in Huay Tong. As a Catholic teacher he taught evening classes in the church to three groups of villagers: children, youth and adults. He also taught them how to read and write in Karen and Thai and how to translate the languages from one to another. After three years he was appointed as a government teacher at a school in the neighbouring village Naung Tau. There Kru Tip taught children arithmetic as well as the Thai and English languages. The teaching was irregular and sometimes children did not show up at all. School lunch was not provided and usually, children brought their lunch—rice and *misato*—from their home. There were no uniforms and no distribution of milk in the afternoon. Nevertheless, every morning the children and their teachers sang the national anthem and on Fridays they sang the King's song.

Taking up his new appointment did not prevent Kru Tip from continuing teaching at night in Huay Tong. The two-year appointment in Naung Tau was followed by another two-year appointment in Mae Sapok, a three-year appointment in Tung Luang and five years in Huay I Khan. During this time, teacher Kru Tip was employed in the Public Welfare Department and even met King Bhumibol. Teacher Kru Tip used his position and personal contacts for the benefit of the wider community. Thanks to teacher Kru Tip's intervention with the Mae Wang district officer, in

1973 Huay Tong became the first highland village with a government school. There were three classrooms, but not enough teachers. Kru Tip would therefore write on the blackboard for one group and while they were copying from the blackboard, he would move to the next group. His former student Maliwan remembers how Kru Tip attended to each child, guiding them carefully by their arms and showing them how to write (Suksawad, 11 June 2008).

For Pav Di the missionary school in Mae Pon was the starting point for an adult career in education. He attended Mae Pon School between the ages 9 and 12 years. Afterwards he made the transition to the prestigious public school Montfort College in Chiang Mai. This high school was run by Catholic missionaries and attended by largely Buddhist children from the upper echelons of Thai society. He obtained scholarships because he was talented and eager to study. In 2007 Pav Di obtained a doctoral degree in Social Science from Chiang Mai University and worked as the Regional Director of the Indigenous Knowledge and Peoples Network (IKAP) and the Inter Mountain Peoples Education and Culture in Thailand Association (IMPECT). Through IMPECT he has implemented local curriculum projects since 1995 to communicate the importance of local curricula to government agencies. The contents of these study programmes centred on agriculture, tradition, customs and livelihood. According to an evaluation of educational projects of ethnic minorities in the hills of northern Thailand, the IMPECT curriculum project had such an effect that local curricula entered the formal education system. As an outcome, several young people enhanced their literacy in such a way that they obtained urban jobs or scholarships to higher education. Pav Di's educational pathway exemplifies the way education is a gift that young persons—in this case Pav Di—receive from elders in their community through informal learning as well as through teachers at modern institutions like the Thai primary school, Montfort College and Chiang Mai University. Receiving the gift of education in such an abundant way encouraged Pav Di to reciprocate with similar generosity. He became active in working towards the dissemination of cultural heritage and access to formal education for Karen children.

Girls' education and development received particular attention through the Baan Marina project. Baan Marina is a boarder school for vocational skill training of ethnic minority girls in northern Thailand. The educational project started in Mae Pon and arrived in 1965 in Chiang Mai. At the time of its inception, the project welcomed girls at around the age of 15. Usually these girls had already finished primary education and spent some time at their parental home helping with household tasks before they arrived at Baan Marina for vocational training, such as sewing and dressmaking. In 2009, with the rising value of schooling and formal education, 15-year-old girls often arrived directly after graduation from lower secondary school. Whilst learning practical skills at Baan Marina, increasing numbers of girls continue their formal education at free weekend classes offered at nearby Buddhist monasteries. With the help of the religious sisters, from the Order Misioneras del Sagrado Corazón de Jesús y María (Missionaries of the Sacred Heart of Jesus and May) students at Baan Marina often found work as dressmakers and started earning money to help their parents and families. Sr. Chelo confirms that very often the girls had a lot of responsibility vis-à-vis their parental households. Their income is used for buying land or motorbikes, sometimes even for paying for their brother's schooling (Interview, Garcia, 13 July 2009). The next chapter draws attention to schools as spaces of inclusion and marginalization.

Bibliography

Ariès, P. 1996. *Centuries of childhood.* London: Pimlico.

Ba, V. 1964. The beginnings of western education in Burma—The catholic effort. *Journal of Burma Research Society* 47(2): 287–324.

Ball, J. 2011. *Enhancing learning of children from diverse language backgrounds: Mother tongue-based bilingual or multilingual education in the early years.* Paris: UNESCO.

Bigandet, P.A. 1887. *An outline of the history of the catholic Burmese mission: From the year 1720 to 1887.* Rangoon: The Hanthawaddy Press.

Buadaeng, K. 2003. *Buddhism, Christianity and the ancestors: Religion and pragmatism in a Skaw Karen community of North Thailand.* Chiang Mai: Social Research Institute\Chiang Mai University.

Cunningham, H. 1991. *The Children of the poor: Representations of childhood since the seventeenth century.* Oxford: Blackwell.

Emmons, C.F. 1964. *The Ghekhu by Paolo Manna, Translated and Annotated.* Thesis, Urbana. Illinois.

Furnivall, J.S. 1957. *An introduction to the political economy of Burma.* Rangoon: Peoples Literature Committee & House.

Garcia, C. 2009. Interview, 13 July 2009.

Gomane, A. 1964. Suan Tchet Rin. *Feuilles Missionaires: Bulletin trimestriel de la Mission des PP. de Betharram au Siam* 37: 10–13.

Griffini, M. 1781. *Della Vita di Monsignor Gio: Maria Percoto della Congregazione di S. Paolo Missionario Ne' Regni di Ava e di Pegu.* Udine: Fratelli Gallici.

Hall Hunt, R. 2005. *Bless god and take courage. The Judson history and legacy.* Valley Forge: The Judson Press.

Hayami, Y. 2004. *Between hills and plains: Power and practice in socio-religious dynamics among the Karen.* Kyoto: Kyoto University Press and Trans Pacific Press.

Howard, R.L. 1931. *Baptists in Burma.* Philadelphia: The Judson Press.

Keyes, C.F. 1991. The proposed world of the school: Thai villagers' entry into a bureaucratic state system. In *Reshaping local worlds: Formal education and cultural change in rural southeast Asia*, ed. C.F. Keyes, 89–130. New Haven: Yale Center for International and Area Studies.

Keyes, C.F. 2003. The politics of 'Karen-ness' in Thailand. In *Living at the edge of Thai society. The Karen in the highlands of northern Thailand*, ed. C.O. Delang, 210–218. London: Curzon.

King, A. 1835. *Memoir of George Dana Boardman, late missionary to Burma.* Boston: Gould Kendall & Lincoln.

Lall, M., and A. South. 2014. Comparing models of Non-state ethnic education in Myanmar: The Mon and Karen national education regimes. *Journal of Contemporary Asia* 44: 298–321.

Loades, D.M. 2006. *Elizabeth I.* London: Hambledon Continuum.

Locke, J. 1699. *Some thoughts concerning education.* London: Black Swann.

Luzzi, C. 2015. Interview, 26 March 2015.

Maniratanavongsiri, C. 2008. Interview, 11 February 2008.

Marshall, H.I. 1997. *The Karen people of Burma. A study in anthropology and ethnology.* Bangkok: White Lotus.

May, H., B. Kaur, and L. Prochner. 2014. *Empire education and indigenous childhoods: Nineteenth- century missionary infant schools in three British colonies.* Farnham: Ashgate.

Metro, R. 2013. Postconflict history curricula revision as an 'intergroup encounter' promoting interethnic reconciliation among burmese migrants and refugees in Thailand. *Comparative Education Review* 57(1): 145–168.

Missionaires, Feuilles. 1970. Me Phon. *Feuilles Missionaires: Bulletin trimestriel de la Mission des PP. de Betharram au Siam* 60: 10.

Montfort College. 2015. *School history.* http://www.montfort.ac.th/english/history.html. Accessed 7 June 2015.

Myint Swe, J. 2014. *The cannon soldiers of Burma.* Toronto: We Make Books.

Rogers, B. 2004. *A land without evil. Stopping the genocide of Burma's Karen people.* Oxford: Monarch Books.

Rousseau, J.J. 1893. *Rousseau's Émile: Or, Treatise on education.* Abridged, translated, and annotated by William H. Payne. London: Sidney Appleton.

Sangermano, V. 1893. *The Burmese Empire a hundred years ago as described by Father Sangermano. With an introduction and notes by John Jardine.* Westminster: Archibald Constable and Company.

Smith, M. 1999. *Burma. Insurgency and the politics of ethnicity.* Dhaka: University Press.

Socarras, C.J. 1966. The Portuguese in lower Burma: Filipe de Brito de Nicote. *Luso-Brazilian Review* 3(2): 3–24.

Suksawad, Kru Tip. 2008. Interview, 11 June 2008.

Symes, M. 1800. *An account of an embassy to the Kingdom of Ava, sent by the Governor-General of India, in the year 1795.* By Michael Symes, Esq. Major in his Majesty's 76th Regiment. London, 1800. Eighteenth Century Collections Online. Gale. University of Oxford. Accessed 5 June 2015.

Trakansuphakon, P. 2008. Interview, 15 July 2008.

Trakansuphakon, P. 2015. Email, 9 July 2015.

Turner, D. 2015. *The old boys. The decline and rise of the public school.* New Haven: Yale University Press.

Wyatt, D.K. 1969. *The politics of reform in Thailand: Education in the reign of King Chulalongkorn.* New Haven: Yale University Press.

Wyeth, W.N. 1891. *The wades. A memorial.* Philadelphia: C.J. Krehbiel & Co.

Zelizer, V.A. 1985. *Pricing the priceless child: The changing social value of children.* New York: Basic Books.

CHAPTER 4

Schools as Sites of Inclusion and Marginalization

Modern education and the sociopolitical inclusion of marginalized communities are interrelated. As outlined in Chap. 3, the modern education system in Thailand was established alongside other modern institutions during the period of early state formation at the end of the nineteenth century (Keyes 1991a: 89). Likewise, Chayan Vaddhanaphuti (1991) analyses how changing modes of production are related to changing patterns of learning in rural Thailand. He explains how the penetration of the state into local communities intensified when the state started the First National Economic and Social Development Plan in 1960. The aim of this plan was to accelerate rural development through an expanding cash economy and a state-sponsored school system (Vaddhanaphuti 1991: 154). As in other nation states, Thai state schools promoted vernacular standardized languages-of-state. This national language was imposed over regional dialects. The dialects, in turn, became signifiers of locality. Therefore, use of local language can enhance or diminish socio-economic and political status and participation within the wider geographic space of the nation:

When people use standard Thai, there is often implicit acceptance of the authority of the Thai state. This acceptance is evident in the precise use of particular pronouns and polite ending forms that situate the speakers within the status system validated by the state (Keyes 1991b: 112).

In addition to language, state-schools in Thailand also introduced new standards of punctuality, hygiene and adult-child interactions. Schools are also the places where children develop civic and religious values such as

P. Jolliffe, *Learning, Migration and Intergenerational Relations*,
DOI 10.1057/978-1-137-57218-9_4

loyalty to the King, the nation and the Buddhist religion (Vaddhanaphuti 1991: 164). The expansion of rural education since the 1970s has led to an increased demand for teachers and teacher training. Becoming a teacher thus became a means of upward social mobility for young people with rural background. However, teachers also felt that teaching was not economically rewarding. Many young teachers preferred assignments in urban areas and felt disappointed when they were instead sent to serve in rural places. Moreover, the school curriculum is not sensitive to the needs of rural children. Instead of preparing them to become competent agricultural producers, schools encourage children to aspire for high education and white-collar occupations which they may never carry out (Vaddhanaphuti 1991: 159–161). My research concurs with the work of Keyes and Vaddhanaphuti (1991), in that I found that Thai schools remain a site of contradiction.

Huay Tong and Its School

Until the late 1970s, children in Huay Tong migrated for education to Mae Pon school. In 1966, the first village school was established and Betharram missionaries sent the teacher Tip, we discussed in the last chapter, to Huay Tong. As mentioned earlier, Tip was one of the first physically handicapped children educated in Mae Pon. As the first Karen teacher in Huay Tong, he taught children arithmetic as well as the Thai and English languages. In 1973, Huay Tong children started attending a Thai government school in neighbouring Baan Naung Tau. Teaching and school attendance were irregular. The children commuted once or twice per week to school and often found the teacher absent. Five years later, in 1978, Huay Tong received its first Thai government school built by the Buddhist Phra Dhammacharik Project. In 1979, the school received the official name Baan Huay Tong School and was put under the directive of the Office of Secondary Schools, Amphur Sanpathong.

In January 2008, Huay Tong school counted 301 students, 15 Thai teachers and 2 employees. Thai government education was available for kindergarten levels 1 and 2, primary school (bprà-tŏm) grades 1–6 as well as secondary school (máttayom) grades 1–3. A range of institutional networks provide personal connections between highland villages and lowland schools. Compared to the past, students and parents were generally now more familiar with the national education system and better equipped to navigate the world outside their living areas.

Since 1999, the school has had a girl dormitory and since 2008 a boy dormitory for students whose villages are too distant for daily travel. At the time of fieldwork, Huay Tong was the only Karen village in Mae Win offering schooling beyond primary education. Therefore, the village had become a local destination for children's migration for education. In 2008, almost half of the students at the post-primary level commuted from surrounding villages: namely, Huai Kiang (two kilometres away), Huay Khan (two kilometres away), Naung Tau (four kilometres), Huay Kao Lip (five kilometres), Tung Luang (eight kilometres), Huay Yen (ca. 14 kilometres away), Naung Mun Tan (ca. 20 kilometres away), and Mae Ta La (Mae Chaem district). Moreover, 15 toddlers commuted daily to Huay Tong kindergarten from neighbouring Huay I Khan village. With the exception of Mae Ta La, the villages are situated in Mae Wang district. Those living in nearby villages commute daily on motorbikes or in collective car transports funded by the local administration. Those whose home villages are located further away stay in school dormitories or enter into seasonal foster arrangements. They only return to their home villages during weekends or school breaks. In 2009, 22 girls and 13 boys from Tun Luang, Huay Giang, Naung Mun Tan and Huay Yen were staying in the dormitories. They were supervised by female teachers who stayed on campus during the week. According to their teacher, the students were responsible for school and personal maintenance. This remark puts moral value on children's work and indicates that formal education and children's activities are not separated in rural Thailand.

After primary school, the Karen children move on to lower secondary school, which is also available in the village. In 2008, 27 out of 30 primary school graduates stayed in Huay Tong for secondary education. The remaining three were ordained as novices for post-primary education in the Buddhist Wat Srisoda in Chiang Mai. Graduation from lower secondary school is again a major turning point. After nine years of basic education, most youth aspired to temporally leave their villages for higher secondary education or apprenticeships. Most students made an educational transition to high school in the lowlands or sought paid employment with the Royal Agricultural Project. The majority of boys continue in Sanpathong Agricultural College or went to St Joseph minor seminary. Girls tended to go to Ban Kad high school, Santisuk school or Coeli school in Chiang Mai. Karen children's growing migration for education prompted increasing collaboration between households, Thai government schools and religious and non-governmental bodies. The support of religious networks was different than in the past, reflecting the changing needs of increasing numbers of Karen students who aspire to higher formal education. In spite of these educational opportunities, there are also challenges related to the Thai state-school system and its values.

Introducing Modern Values

As outlined above, modern education introduces to local settings globalized ideas of and practices associated with 'development' and 'modernity'. These new sets of practices may differ from traditional learning. Anthropological research highlights the role of Thai state schools in educating children into becoming national citizens (e.g. Keyes 1991a; Vaddhanaputhi 1991). My research adds to this body of research and shows that also among the Karen in Huay Tong the promotion of modern education through the local Thai school is not a straightforward process. Instead, the state school and associated modern values create dissonance and contestation along political, economic and generational lines within the village community as well as within individual households.

For instance, government education introduces modern understandings of human maturation. These legal and psychological ideas of child development contrast local practices. Teachers are challenged to expand their ideas through weekend workshops on alternative teaching methods, which provide ideas of how to bring more excitement and creativity into their teaching. Through this training, teachers become acquainted with psychological notions of child development, which they contrast to traditional Karen practices of childrearing. For instance, one teacher presented me with a leaflet on child brain development. He emphasized that nursery school is meant to stimulate children in this respect 'because the parents cannot develop their children'. This promotion of institutional infant care contrasts with local views on early child development. In the eyes of Karen villagers, it seems more advantageous if a mother can stay at home with her child, rather than having to take it with her to work or leave it in the nursery. This preference speaks of socio-economic status differences among the Karen. As explained in the Introduction, according to the Karen myth of the lost book agricultural work has less value than formal education. Therefore, young Karen adults who participated in my research felt sorry for mothers who had to 'work hard' and took their children with them to the rice fields. By contrast, the possibility of staying at home with her child means that a woman does not have to 'work hard' in either a subsistence or cash economy. Institutional care in the nursery also reveals intra-Karen socio-economic differences related to economic changes in agricultural production. During fieldwork in 2009, I found working parents drop off their children at the village nursery at 7:30 am. They were expected to pick them up at 4:00 pm. Children whose mothers were engaged in wage labour at the Royal Project seemed to attend nursery to a greater extent. For example, Tik—whose mother works for the Royal Project—went to the nursery when she was two-years old. In contrast, Pit—who comes from one of the richest families in Huay Tong—never attended nursery school and went straight to kindergarten at the age of four. Pit's parents do not have to engage in wage labour and therefore had more time for childcare.

Modern ideas of personal hygiene are promoted by Thai state schools. In accordance with modern school regulations, Thai school teachers critique Karen practices of hygiene and body care. School regulations expect girls' hair to be no longer than below the ears and boys to have their hair very short. These regulations differ for children in the plains, especially at private schools where girls are allowed to keep their hair long. Thai teachers explained the obligation for short hair in the mountains with reference to ethnic minority children being 'lazy to wash' and more prone to catch lice during the cold season. Therefore, during term time, students at Huay Tong school had a monthly haircut. Those with richer parents went to a hairstylist in a village further down in Mae Win. Teenage girls often cut their own hair or helped one another, while those who did not receive a haircut at home had their hair shortened by a teacher in the school compound. Moreover, teachers paid meticulous attention to children's body care, monitoring the state of their nails and clothes regularly. If children appeared in what was not considered hygienic, they were asked whether they took a bath the other day. Teachers felt that children often responded to this question with a lie because they feared scolding or punishment. There may be several reasons children did not conform to the standards set by the government school. Teachers claimed children in kindergarten and primary school could take care of themselves and relied on their parents, and some adults argue that certain parents did not care well for their children. One teacher complained Karen parents did not care sufficiently for their children because of their workload in the fields. However, my own exchanges with the children suggest that they know how to take care of themselves but do not necessarily want to conform to school standards. Participatory research exercises I conducted with children of different age groups suggest that girls and boys at around the age of seven can wash themselves, as well as change and wash their clothes by themselves. For example, in his life course drawing (Fig. 4.1) the 14-year-old boy, Fee, depicted himself washing and drying clothes at the age of 7 years.

The Thai school promotes time discipline and economic efficiency. These ideas may be in dissonance with local patterns of timing activities according to diurnal and seasonal changes. Indeed time budgeting is a rather new idea. In the Karen language there is no word for 'time'. Instead, Karen people use in their own Karen language Thai loan words when discussing general notions of 'time', when they measure the hours of the clock, or when they say that some activity was a 'waste of time'. In addition, there exists a discrepancy between the time-use priorities of the socio-economic groups of farmers and bureaucrats. These differences are often ethnicized, i.e. explained with references to 'ethnic' and not 'economic' differences. For example, teachers tended to regard people in Huay Tong as lacking a sense of time discipline, being carefree, doing as they please and taking life easy. They felt that Karen people got up late and only at appointments when they want to. This lead some teachers to question Karen peoples' work ethos: 'lazy to learn, lazy to work'. However,

Fig. 4.1 Seven-year-old Karen boy can wash his clothes by himself, June 2008

rather than being lazy, my research suggests that school demands on children's and parents' time use may be in dissonance with seasonal labour requirements in the fields. Parents may be unable to attend teacher-parent meetings during the day when they have to work in the fields. Indeed, because of their working obligations in the rice fields, many parents found it impossible to attend school meetings, or to wait for teachers to visit their homes. In the eyes of teachers, this amounted to parental lack of interest in their children's educational affairs.

My study furthermore suggests that Karen children themselves were not always happy to adapt to the rigid timetable in school. During fieldwork in Huay Tong I sometimes found boys and girls 'escaping' from school, preferring to roam the countryside or hide in the village mango trees. Moreover, Karen and Thai adults sometimes underestimated children's preference for working activities. In the eyes of Thai teachers, students who dropped out of school and started working were 'lazy'. Children's preference for work was 'not so good' because 'when we study we can make good work'. It seems that to this day, highland subsistence farming is conventionally related to rural poverty and ignorance associated with the legend of the lost book described in the introduction.

Verbal and Non-verbal Communication

At school, integration occurs when Karen children learn skills that help them to participate in local, regional and international communities, institutions and markets. Indeed as outlined above, since their inception in rural Thailand, state schools have prepared children for future citizenship. The teaching of literacy and numeracy prepares them for economic life, while the spatial organization of school compounds itself has been described as reflecting general architectonic power structures of administrative buildings in Thailand:

> When Thai children go to school, they enter a spatial culture that itself serves as a model of the state. The interactions that students have with teachers, as well as those teachers have with villagers more generally, also anticipate in form and significance the relationships that villagers have with representatives of the state (Keyes 1991b: 90).

Indeed during fieldwork for this book, the author also found that by the time they attended kindergarten, Karen children had learnt the characters of the Thai script through singing and playing. Despite these preparations, however, most children continued to struggle with reading and writing Thai throughout primary school. Children's difficulties written language were evident throughout the research process. For example, during participatory research exercises I observed how the children distributed work amongst themselves, In this way, I found that it was always the same girl and boy who were in charge of writing because it was only them who felt confident to write in front of everyone. At school, Karen children were to respect national symbols through the three pillars (Buddhism, Royalty and the Flag). Thus, Thai national schooling enhanced Karen children's participation in society, especially through the teaching and learning of the Thai language and the inculcation of national values. Lack of literacy in the national language—as well as ignorance of culturally valued body language—severely restricted ethnic minority peoples' agency and opportunities in the country. For these reasons, Karen parents in Mae Wang, Chiang Mai, generally supported their children's introduction to Thai sociocultural values and manners at school. They knew that in order to engage with national and international institutions, such as access to higher education or jobs in the Thai labour market, children needed to be able to show respect for mainstream Thai culture and national symbols. Karen children's own perception of the close association between the state school and Thai national culture transpired during participatory research exercises: in their drawings, the school building is often adorned with the national flag. In most schools, children are introduced to the Thai language and national symbols from nursery onwards. At my fieldwork site in Mae Wang, a Karen caregiver often supervised children. At this stage of early education, children spoke Karen and were not required to eat at a table. Instead, children had their lunch sitting on the floor, just as they would have done in their Karen homes. At the same time, the caregiver practised the Thai and English alphabets with them through games and concentration tasks. Furthermore, the caregiver taught children respect for Thai national symbols, such as the flag, the national anthem and the King. Like their older peers in the school compound, children in the nursery assembled in the morning to hoist the flag and sing national songs. By the time they attended kindergarten, Karen children have typically learnt the characters of the Thai script through singing and playing. However, most children could not practise Thai at home and therefore continued to struggle with reading and writing Thai throughout primary school. Children who wanted to read and write in their Karen mother tongue, needed to find learning opportunities outside school, like the IMPECT curriculum project mentioned Chap. 3. In Christian Karen villages, catechists volunteered to teach children how to read and write in Karen. Classes took place during the evening within the church or in the house of the catechist. Some children also decided to migrate to Mae Pon School where a one-year curriculum of Karen language was taught (Sanri, interview, 22 March 2008).

Non-verbal communication was also taught at school. In Thailand, Karen children were introduced to the *maa-ra-yaat Thai*. The *maa-ra-yaat Thai* is a code of good social behaviour, including all kinds of subtleties of verbal and non-verbal behaviour. It prescribes how to show respect for intergenerational relations and status differences, through body language and other aspects of social interaction. For example, when passing by a teacher, students have to lower their upper body and greet them with a proper salutation. Similarly, younger students are expected to show respect to their older peers and to obey them in both the village and the school. Mastery of these manners is associated with maintenance of social order and discipline. By the same token, ignorance of *maa-ra-yaat Thai* can have awkward consequences when interacting with Thai people. Buddhist-Thai mainstream society instructs children from infancy onwards in the gradual mastery of this code of conduct, through their parents, teachers and monks. Typically, Thai students also learn from their teachers and parents about the *maa-ra-yaat Thai*. Yet, because Karen culture does not require the young to constantly use the same manners as lowland children do, at the time of fieldwork highland children struggled with mastering this body language. Unfamiliarity with socioculturally valued body language, in turn, created dissonance and misunderstanding between Thai and Karen people.

During fieldwork I frequently observed teachers scorning the reproduction of home culture in the classroom. Hence, what was normal at home was considered awkward behaviour at school. For example, a teacher Sun complained: ‘They shout together. Their parents don’t teach them about good behaviour. Not the same in the city’. She described students who would sit on their chairs with their knees high: ‘I scold them, but their parents do the same’. Teachers tended to frame dissonances in behaviour in ethnic terms, explaining that Karen behaviour differs, for example, from Hmong or northern Thai behaviour. Participation in school events during 2008 and 2009 confirmed the Karen people’s relaxed attitude towards showing respect for national Thai symbols. For example, the importance of mastering Thai Buddhist non-verbal language was highlighted during the National Teacher's Day on 12 June in Thailand. On the annual Teacher's Day, students have to show deference to the Buddha, the King and their teachers. On a stage, a Buddha shrine was placed with the Thai flag and a picture of the Thai monarch. All the teachers were seated next to this arrangement. Students climbed onto the stage in groups, prostrated themselves in front of the sacred arrangement, and then proceeded to bow in front of their teachers. All seemed well. However, after the performance, during lunchtime in the teachers'canteen, the teachers expressed strong emotions when speaking about students' performances, ranging from anger to disappointment and sadness. According to the teachers, the young people had not properly paid their respects. Rather than honouring the Buddha, the monarch and their teachers, they seemed to the teachers to be mocking these authorities. Even teachers who were usually sympathetic to Karen children's difficulties with combining different cultures insisted that what had happened on the day was lamentable, and they expressed concerns for the students' future outside the village. Therefore, notwithstanding state school efforts for national integration, Karen children experienced educational marginalization because of the difference between the sociocultural values of their home and school.

School and Inequality

Notwithstanding state school efforts for children's socio-political integration, schools are also sites of social dissonances. Karen children continue to grow up learning according to a standardized curriculum with little sensitivity for their sociocultural and historical background. Students are called by their Thai names and are only allowed to speak Thai in class. Children are required to strip off their Karen names and adopt Thai names. The use of any language except Central Thai is forbidden. Concealing their linguistic diversity is probably the most immediate and defensive reaction in settings dominated by ethnic Thai people. Methods of concealment include feigning shyness of speech, falling completely silent and being secretive about one's place of origin. Karen people becoming shy and silent in a situation where 'others' are in the majority, both in the lowlands and in the highlands, is something I observed several times when accompanying Karen adults to the plains. In the lowlands, it can take time for Karen people to reveal their geographic background to mainstream Thai people. Teacher Tik described her Karen students as shy and timid. In particular those who were studying in lowland high schools are careful to only gradually reveal their identity: 'If they speak good Thai, they will never tell first 'I am Karen from Huay Tong'. But once they are friends they will tell. If it is not necessary, they don't speak. They are silent' (Teacher Tik, interview, 27 July 2009). But other teachers suspected that Karen students use their mother tongue or fall completely silent in order to conceal shyness and to avoid being mocked by their Thai peers.

At the moment of fieldwork, teaching methods remained largely insensitive to the necessities of students whose mother tongue differs from the Thai language spoken in classrooms. Educated Karen adults were concerned about the quality of Thai language teaching. They mentioned to me worries about Thai teachers not being motivated or having the right aptitude. According to them, in the past, Karen teachers educated in Mae Pon were better equipped to teach the national language. For example, 31-year-old Naw La—who holds a bachelor's degree—wondered in 2008 why there are no Karen teachers, unlike during her childhood. She was of the opinion that Karen teachers taught the Thai language better than current Thai teachers. She adds that because of the poor teaching some people were even unable to read and write in Thai (Naw La, interview, 12 May 2008). Indeed Thai teachers in different villages were often poorly prepared to teach in culturally diverse classrooms. This was particularly true of the older generation of teachers. Unfortunately, these were often the teachers who at the end of their careers were sent to teach in the highlands. This issue was raised by Maliwan, the local parents' representative at Huay Tong school, in a letter to the school director. In it, she complained that the standard of Huay Tong school was far below the national average and remarked on the following issues: teachers should arrive punctually in the morning, just as they asked of the children; time in the classrooms should be fully used; and teachers should inform parents if children are not coming to school, because only in collaboration can teachers and parents improve the situation. Finally, she argued that more young teachers were required as they would be more motivated than older teachers who were close to retirement (Kasedsookjai, interview, 18 March 2008). Indeed schools in the highlands generally lower teaching quality than in the plains. When making the transition to high school in the plains, therefore, students often needed to make additional efforts to catch up with their new classroom standards. Even if they were excellent students in the mountains, their performance tended to be far below those who attended lower secondary school in the lowlands.

Bullying and ethnic stereotyping is common, especially at government schools in the lowlands. Remembering her studies in Ban Kad during the early 1990s, Naw Hpaiv Naiv recalls: 'Thai people looked down on Karen. They "liked bullying" calling them "*chaokhăo*" [hill people] and "dirty" (Naw Hpaiv Naiv, interview, 9 June 2008). At the time of research, ethnic stereotypes are often conveyed through jokes and seemingly benign comments. Thai teachers and classmates brought them into the classroom. For example, I frequently heard teachers making general comparisons between different ethnic groups, describing 'the Karen' as being 'messy in their house', 'dirty', 'getting up late', with no social rules governing their everyday behaviour or 'taking it always easy'. Thai schools' efforts to instil values of citizenship and national belonging were creating dissonances. On the one hand they helped children with integration into national society and economy. On the other hand, state school attendance rendered children more sensitive of their political marginality within mainstream Thai society.

Moreover, socio-economic inequality between middle-class Thai consumer culture and Karen highland villages were evident in Thai government schools. In Huay Tong, kindergarten teachers used leaflets from city supermarkets to teach children the Thai language and widen their general knowledge. From primary school onwards, teachers took students on excursions to the lowlands, such as to hot springs, the zoological garden in Chiang Mai or the famous Buddhist temple on Mount Doi Suthep. Also a shopping mall visit was an integral part of such excursions. During fieldwork I found that children enjoyed excursions to shopping malls. It was an exciting event, which was very different from their everyday lives in the highland villages. Nevertheless, the confrontation with urban consumer culture highlighted the economic inequalities between Karen children as well as between highlanders and lowlanders. For example, talking about shopping mall visits in Chiang Mai, Panida explained that she liked to look at things but 'cannot buy because there is no money'. Karen parents also complained to me that high school canteens in the lowlands were expensive and only provided small food portions insufficient to meet the hunger of teenage boys. For instance, speaking about her 15-year-old son's transition from Huay Tong school to Sanpathong Agricultural Polytechnic College, Fee's mother worried that 'They eat and are not full' (Naw Raiv Di, interview, 18 July 2009). Still hungry, Fee and his friends had to go outside the school to buy food.

Thai teachers also emphasized the socio-economic differences between Karen village life and the lowlands. Throughout my fieldwork in Huay Tong school, teachers were anxious to point out the status differences between northern Thai students in the lowlands and the Karen children I studied in Huay Tong. For example, they stressed the difficulty of organizing overland school excursions in Huay Tong, explaining that Karen parents had less money than lowlanders to support these trips. A three-day trip to Bangkok and a nearby beach costed roughly 500 baht per student in 2008. In lowland schools, parents paid this once, whereas in Huay Tong parents make monthly contributions to a collective depot according to what they were able to afford. When Thai teachers organized bus journeys rather than train travel, this was because on the coach 'everyone is equal', while trains operate with a class system. The teachers, therefore, avoided having to adapt to the lower socio-economic position of highlanders most of whom could only afford a third-class ticket.

Socio-economic status differences between children themselves can also be seen in schools. School transitions to the lowlands insert Karen youth into Thai lowland society where people are generally wealthier, own different products and have different consumption practices. Rural parents may underestimate the influence and pressure of peer comparisons and blame TV commercials for their children's rising consumerist aspirations. For example, 12-year-old Pit migrated in May 2008 from Huay Tong to lower secondary education at St Joseph school in Sampran. A few months after the transition, he mentioned to his mother on the telephone his need for new underwear. Throughout primary school in Huay Tong, he had been using underwear bought for 20 baht from a sale in his mother's village shop. At the minor seminary, Pit felt that these were not good enough anymore and asked his mother to buy men's underwear from a well-known brand costing over 100 baht per item. Pit's mother attributed his new desires to the influence of TV commercials. Although she was from a wealthy household in Huay Tong, she found the request exaggerated and her advice to her son was 'do not worry, none can see it' (Naw Wiv La, interview, 18 July 2009). His mother probably overlooked the fact that boys share sleeping rooms and changing rooms for sport which offer plenty of opportunities for comparison.

The reputation of particular schools is also a socio-economic status symbol. School prestige is important and can enhance or mitigate children's social status. Students worry about the value and the social prestige of their future school. As a public welfare school, Santisuk school is known to be an institution for 'poor people'. The low prestige of Santisuk school worried the young girl Panida and the boy De. Before their transition to high school, they eagerly searched for positive comments on their future school. In the course of applying in person to Santisuk, De turned to me, commenting that the school compound 'is pretty, isn't it?' Struggling with her disappointment at being unable to attend the school that was her first choice , Panida also asked for my confirmation that Santisuk was like Ban Kad. She also sought my opinion on which school was prettier. Karen children seem aware that education is a means to boost or undermine their social status among their peers and within their households and village communities.

Encouraging Diversity Through School Projects

As outlined above, challenges to Karen students' equal access to modern education remain. Although at the time of fieldwork government education in Thailand was generally free, there are various unseen costs involved in children's education, such as stationery, school uniforms, transport and dormitory places. Schools and village communities were therefore making efforts of fundraising to improve school buildings and the welfare of needy students. For example, during fieldwork in Huay Tong I learned that the Japanese NGO Network Harmony and the Christian charity Jesuit Social Service supported the educational needs of the Karen children in Mae Wang. As part of these programmes, the directors of the Japanese Network Harmony Foundation and the Jesuit Social Service paid periodic visits to Huay Tong. They visited schools and met with Thai teachers and Karen students and their parents. The whole procedure of hosting foreign benefactors took place in an organized form and involves the collaborative participation of Karen children and adults as well as Thai teachers. Participant observation of these processes revealed the cultural diversity as well as the socio-economic inequality underlying these relationships. In the following section I compare the visit of the Japanese and Spanish delegation of benefactors to Huay Tong village and the school.

In February, 2008, the Japanese delegation headed by the vice president of Network Harmony Foundation, visited Huay Tong to inaugurate a newly built dormitory. They arrived in the evening, spent a night in the school compound and left the following day. One month later, in mid-March 2008, a Jesuit delegation from Bangkok including the Spanish director of the Jesuit Social Service met the families of Karen children who participated to the scholarship programme in Huay Tong village.

Karen and Thai people in Huay Tong spent a lot of time preparing for both visits. A week before the arrival of the Japanese guests, students and teachers were still busy finalizing the dormitory and decorating the area around it with flowers. The day before the guests' arrival, the whole school was in a commotion. The library had been transformed into a dining and sleeping hall for the visitors. On the inauguration day, the school compound was in an exceptional state. Regular teaching was suspended and the entire day was dedicated to the visit. Students were exhorted to wear their traditional Karen clothes, and teachers insisted more rigorously than usual on maintaining discipline.

The visit of the Jesuit delegation fell in the first week of the long school summer break. Days before the arrival of the important delegation, Maliwan, a Karen lady and contact person for the local distribution of scholarships, was anxious that everything should proceed well in an orderly manner and without fault. In an effort to gather all the children who receive scholarships, she asked their relatives to gather at her own household on the day of the Jesuit's visit so that the children and their parents would be present on the important occasion. Just like for the Japanese delegation at the Thai school, the students helped preparing Maliwan house.

For the Japanese as well as for the Spanish visitor, local Thai and Karen people made efforts to honour their guests through the preparation of special food. Throughout the visit of the Japanese donors, food preparation was not entrusted to the usual Karen school cook; instead, a senior Thai teacher took responsibility for preparing the food. Similarly, in Maliwan's household, special food was prepared for the Spanish visitors, including a lot of meat, whilst the scholarship children and their parents were served an ordinary and simple Karen dish.

Food consumption therefore mirrors unequal social status relations. At Huay Tong school, a canopy was set up on the compound for the Japanese visitors to have snacks and protect themselves from the sun. Main meals were taken in the library, and food was served according to the hierarchical non-verbal behaviour prescribed in the codified polite manners of the *maa-ra-yâat Thai*. According to the *maa-ra-yâat Thai*, social juniors serve their seniors. So, Thai teachers are usually served by their students. However, during the visit of the Japanese donors, the Thai teachers served their high-ranking guests food, hence emphasizing the visitors' senior status. After the Japanese visitors had started eating their meal, their Thai hosts took places further down the table to eat the same food. The teachers also invited those Karen teenage girls who had helped in serving beverages to join them.

It was a rare moment to see adults and young people of such different Japanese, Thai and Karen background sitting together and sharing a meal.

A similar table order emerged during the Jesuit delegation's lunch at Maliwan's house. The guests were seated at the table outside the shop, visible to all passers-by. They enjoyed their special meal and also tried typical Karen food, while Maliwan and four children from the village community ate the same food inside the house. In contrast, those children who arrived from other villages ate Karen food with their relatives in a separate space in the compound's interior yard. In separating children and adults according to their place of residence and household attachments, social boundaries according to location and political affiliation were evoked.

Gift exchanges symbolized the highlight of Karen children's encounters with the scholarship benefactors. As in other societies when it comes to gifts, the values of the exchanged goods are not commensurable and reflect status differences between donors and recipients (Mauss 1990: 83). The Japanese donors handed symbolic cheques to the Karen girls during the inauguration ceremony of the newly built dormitory, while photos were taken. In 'exchange', the Japanese received the honour of the Thai teachers and Karen students who served and entertained the high-ranking guests. In Maliwan's household, visitors were also paid respect through the service and entertainment. The Jesuit director and his team posed for a picture with the scholarship children, and the Spanish visitors each received a wrapped gift of a hand-woven Karen bag from the girls who handed the gifts to the seated guests. In accordance with the *maa-ra-yâat Thai*, the girls moved on their knees towards the benefactors who were seated on chairs. In this kneeling position, they bowed down and handed the wrapped bags to their guests.

Interestingly, the Japanese and Spanish guests differed in their interactions with the locals. The Japanese donors appeared more detached from the Karen children than the Spanish visitors. Throughout their visit, the hierarchy between Japanese guests and their Thai and Karen hosts was maintained. For example, no mixture of food occurred. They observed cultural and social distance with Karen children, neither sharing food nor wrapping themselves with Karen-made fabrics. The head of the delegation also demonstrated her high status vis-à-vis the Thai teachers by deliberately breaching the school's non-smoking policy. Despite a general non-smoking policy in government buildings throughout Thailand, the Japanese director lit a cigarette in the library without any intervention from the teachers. Teachers' tolerance of the Japanese director's smoking evidenced their humbling themselved before the Japanese benefactors. In contrast, the Spaniards' exchange with Karen children was more immediate and mutual. They entered the local Karen household, ate Karen food and gratefully received Karen bags.

Across Thailand, children's dancing and singing performances accompany most major events at different places, such as temples, night bazaars, schools, etc. Also in Huay Tong, encounters between Karen children and scholarship benefactors included entertainment delivered by children. Local children and adults used their cultural heritage as a means to honour their foreign visitors: the wearing of local clothes, the performance of traditional *don* dances and the presenting of locally produced gifts, as well as the exhibiting of polite body language. International scholarship institutions and their representatives are effectively treated as seniors. Cultural difference is highlighted through Karen and regional Thai clothes and dances. Girls usually wear their *hsewa* and perform seasonal group dances related to the rice harvest, while boys tend to perform individually in their *hseigauz*, mostly singing songs about the agricultural circle. For performances at Huay Tong school, the Thai teachers chose four girls to dress up in Lanna (northern Thai) costume and dance typical regional dances. At Huay Tong school, the female teacher who instructed in such dances was a woman from Isan. Isan people usually tended to visualize themselves as a distinct ethnic group. Therefore, the fact that an Isan woman was instructing Karen girls in northern Thai dances showed how flexible the use of 'ethnicity' is. During the Japanese visit, all students appeared in their home spun clothes. Female toddlers even had to wear their mothers' decorative turbans (*hkòhpè*). As they were not used to wearing turbans, the Karen school cook had to keep constantly rearranging their *hkòhpè* behind a barn. While the Japanese were waiting in the school compound, the toddlers had to parade in a seemingly casual way in front of the foreign guests. During lunch, kindergarten children performed aerobics to the national royal anthem, and teenage girls presented local Thai Lanna dances as well as traditional Karen *don* dances.

Children's performance of their cultural heritage had a strong effect on foreign visitors. Seeing Karen children in their home spun clothes engendered nostalgic feelings among the visitors, while the performances stirred enchantment among the spectators because of the cultural exoticism embodied by the schoolgirls. The Japanese director was pleased to see Karen students wearing their traditional dresses and performing their dances and emphasized the importance of ethnic consciousness and cultural heritage. She contrasted these qualities of Karen youth with Japanese students who are less interested in their studies and ethnic identity. The adult niece of the Spanish Jesuit director gave thanks for the Karen hospitality and explained that since childhood she had followed the lives of the Karen children through the photographs her Jesuit uncle sent 'from this far away land' to Spain. Especially captured by girls' traditional clothes, the *hseiwa*, she had always wanted to meet the Karen and was happy the scholarship programme visit offered this opportunity for cultural exchange. The next chapter turns to migration for education and cultural differences between different locations in Karen children's lives.

Bibliography

Kasedsookjai, M. 2008. Interview, 18 March 2008.

Keyes, C.F. 1991a. State schools in rural communities: Reflections on rural education and cultural change in southeast Asia. In *Reshaping local worlds: Formal education and cultural change in rural southeast Asia*, ed. C.F. Keyes, 1–13. New Haven: Yale Center for International and Area Studies.

Keyes, C.F. 1991b. The proposed world of the school: Thai villagers' entry into a bureaucratic state system. In *Reshaping local worlds: Formal education and cultural change in rural southeast Asia*, ed. C.F. Keyes, 89–130. New Haven: Yale Center for International and Area Studies.

Mauss, M. 1990. *The gift. The form and reason for exchange in archaic societies.* London: Routledge.

Naw Hpaiv Naiv. 2008. Interview, 9 June 2008.

Naw La. 2008. Interview, 12 May 2008.

Naw Raiv Di. 2009. Interview, 18 July 2009.

Naw Wiv La. 2009. Interview, 18 July 2009.

Sanri. 2008. Interview, 22 March 2008.

Teacher, Tk. 2009. Interview, 27 July 2009.

Vaddhanaphuti, C. 1991. Social and ideological reproduction in rural Northern Thai schools. In *Reshaping local worlds: Rural education and cultural change in southeast Asia*, ed. C.F. Keyes, 153–173. New Haven: Yale University Southeast Asia Studies.

CHAPTER 5

Migration for Education and Social Inequality

In modern economies young people increasingly migrate for secondary and tertiary education (Boyden and Crivello 2014: 37–38; Froerer 2011). In recent years, anthropological studies explored the effect of children's migration for education on intergenerational relations (for example Ansell and van Blerk 2007: 27; Heissler 2011: 35; Holloway and Valentine 2000; Panelli et al. 2010). Through the lenses of fosterage and child circulation, this chapter analyses the link between migration for education and social inequality.

Migration and social mobility between institutional and geographic settings indicates a shift in the relationship between territory, identity and political affiliation. Concepts like 'home' or 'belonging' are not static but are constantly reproduced and multi-layered. People may develop ideas of 'multi-belonging' and simultaneously experience assimilation and marginalization in relation to space (Chatty 2010: 298–301; Bushin et al. 2007: 79–80; Ni Laoire 2008: 47). Children's ability to migrate for education tells about their social status. For instance, in many countries around the world, gender plays an important role in children's access to education (Crivello 2009; Schildkrout 1978: 129). Importantly, the social category 'gender' always intersects with other forms of social inequality such as birth order, generation, citizenship status as well as household wealth or poverty (Sheba 2005: 24; Wright 2016). Migration itself can encourage a reconfiguration of the intersection between social categories like 'gender' and 'generation'. For example, Huijsman's (2013) research on mothers

P. Jolliffe, *Learning, Migration and Intergenerational Relations*,
DOI 10.1057/978-1-137-57218-9_5

and migrant daughters in rural Laos and Thailand evidences how whether or not women were perceived as 'elderly' depended on their activities rather than their biological age. Because some women cared for their grandchildren in the absence of their migrating daughters (the grandchildren's mothers) they carried out activities typical to a mother rather than a grandmother and were therefore in spite of their age not perceived as 'elderly' (Huijsmans 2013: 1905–1906).

'Ethnicity', too, is a social category which shapes migration for education. In fact, 'ethnicity'—understood as indicating political-economic marginality—is linked to particular spaces and locations. Children's 'ethnicity', then, indicates changing social positions at different locations in the political-economic landscapes (Nayak 2003). Ethnic minority children are considered particularly affected by social contexts marked by a plurality of values and norms. Dissonance arises, for instance, in settings of conflicting social values between ethnic communities and mainstream society. This is particularly relevant for education in multi-ethnic school settings (Beale Spencer and Markstrom-Adams 1990: 301). For example, in my fieldwork setting, movements between institutional and geographic locations impact on 'ethnicity'. Karen children refer to their 'Karen'-ethnicity differently depending on the geographic or institutional location. They wear their ethnic clothes in their highland villages with pride, but try to conceal their ethnicity when studying or working among mainstream Thai people in the lowlands. Migration for education caused a reconfiguration of ethnic categories and encouraged children to develop flexible identities.

This chapter analyses migration for education among the Karen in Thailand, first by explaining the socio-economic structures underlying young peoples' migration for work and education. This is followed by a discussion of how foster families and scholarship programmes regulate children's migration for education. The chapter also discusses how girls' and boys' social status changes as they move between different locations and institutions of learning.

Karen Migration for Work and Education

In the highlands of northern Thailand, agricultural transition and expansion of the cash economy are intimately linked to state development projects and modern schooling. Traditionally, ethnic Karen villagers have been engaging in seasonal subsistence wet rice farming. Wet rice farming tells of the interdependence of households and communities. As outlined in Chap. 1, education in Karen subsistence economy was centred on the socio-cultural learning of skills and technologies, like weaving and ploughing a rice field. The cash economy entered the lives of the ethnic Karen people in Mae Wang through the British teak companies. By the 1930s Karen men and youth were working largely for British logging companies, and from the early twentieth century until the late 1950s they worked for other national logging companies (Elliot 1978: 28). Against the backdrop of the Vietnam War and rising international concern for poppy production in the Mekong area, in 1969 the Thai King established the first 'Royal Projects' in the highlands of northern Thailand. Since the 1960s, the Karen have increasingly migrated to lowland towns for work. A first generation of labour migrants from the highlands arrived in Chiang Mai in 1964 to work at Chiang Mai Radio Station on special 'hill tribe' broadcasts. These migrants also found employment in putting on performance shows for tourists. Their relatives gradually joined them in developing a 'hill tribe handicraft production' trade in Chiang Mai's night bazaars (Buadaeng 2005). Facilitated by infrastructure improvements, the cash economy expanded in the highlands while subsistence agriculture gradually diminished. At the same time, Thai government schools were established in the highlands and increasing numbers of children accessed formal education. Many villages welcomed the expansion of the infrastructure, state schools and inclusion in national development processes: 'Rather than being swamped by commercialism, Karen communities appear to be exploring paths of market oriented diversification that support regularly under-producing paddy and upland rice systems' (Walker 2001: 154–155). Since the 1980s the period of economic growth, mobility between rural and urban areas has increased on a wide scale. Nevertheless, the developmental pace remains uneven. As outlined in this chapter, some villages, like Huay Tong, are well connected to national markets and education systems, while other places, like Mae Ta La, lack access to modern institutions. To access education, households mobilize intergenerational relations within systems of fosterage. During fieldwork, I that these systems of fosterage reveal socio-economic status differences among Karen households in different geographic locations. The specific case study in this chapter highlights how intergenerational relations give meaning to fosterage for Karen children's migration for education.

Schooling and Fosterage

Karen households are generally composed of a nuclear family, and are matrilocal. Women hold a relatively strong position within the family and men are conventionally associated with ritual and public life (Mischung 1984: 75–79). Social relationships are structured according to the principle of seniority: 'Karen frequently talk of their relations with others in terms of kinship, which may be a reference to the real facts of marriage or descent, or may refer to a myth, or may even refer to a close social relationship regardless of genealogical connections' (Kunstadter 1979: 137). Kin networks are mobilized to alleviate household expenditure and support household aspirations to send children to school. Relying on intergenerational and kin relations becomes particularly important when there are no institutionally established ways to exercise charity, for example through the institutional channels of the Catholic Church in Thailand: 'We are a church of piety, chanting, and meditation, but there is little outreach to the poor; in fact, religion stops at the church door. Last Christmas, we had a magnificent choir for Midnight Mass made up mainly for poor people and undocumented immigrants. After the service, we sent them home empty-handed, without even a coffee or a sandwich. Like Christ in the manger' (Boonlue, quoted in Calderisi 2013: 128).

Child circulation and fosterage are therefore an answer to poverty and the absence of modern institutional support. Fosterage and scholarship programmes are about socio-economic interdependence and intergenerational relations within families and communities. Child circulation is a traditional local means for mutual support between related households a way of strengthening social ties, building an effective network that will remain key as children mature into a world of poverty and social constraints: 'Given the importance of family connections and the felt urgency of educating one's children among rural-to-urban migrants, there is an unassailable cultural logic to this practice'(Leinaweaver 2008: 4). Karen children in the highlands of northern Thailand, too, migrate for education. Typically, children's migration for education is enabled through intergenerational relations within families, communities and modern institutions at the local, national and international level. Being a foster child often confers upon children ambiguous social status vis-à-vis other children: on the one hand, in their receiving household, their social status is rather low and they often work harder than children born into the household. On the other hand, foster children's status rises when they return to their native community with new knowledge and skills acquired during their time in the foster community.

On a symbolic level, Karen children growing up outside their own household have a reputation for having high morals and wit. Karen mythology offers many stories of orphans who are deprived of their political-economic household support. Thanks to their high moral character they attract the attention of benevolent supernatural beings who invest the orphan with a share of supernatural power. Thus equipped children often become political heroes capable of outdoing powerful figures such as kings, tigers and administrators (Hinton 1999). At the symbolical level, these stories highlight orphans' integrity as well as their potentially subversive power. Today, this symbolism is mirrored in migrating Karen children's flexible social positioning between geographic and institutional locations.

The socio-economic development of the highlands of northern Thailand followed uneven patterns. As a consequence, some villages, like Mae Ta La in Mae Chaem district, lack access to modern institutions, whilst others like Huay Tong, in Mae Wang district, are well connected to national markets and education systems. Such spatialized inequalities, in turn, explain diversity of childhood transition experiences among the Karen minority people residing at different locations. The Karen village of Mae Ta La is typical of the villages from which poor Karen children migrated for education to richer villages and lowland towns. The village was the home of several children whom the author met during various fieldwork visits between 2007 and 2009. During this time the village was situated in a remote, though beautiful area in the Mae Chaem district of Chiang Mai province. On a slope outside the village there was a little Buddhist temple where villagers regularly gathered for worship, religious teaching and socio-cultural activities. As many as 45 households were spread along a river. By way of comparison, in 2014 Huay Tong village counted 120 households and 586 registered residents.

The infrastructure in Mae Ta La was rather poor. The village was not connected to paved roads and was inaccessible during the rainy season. There was no running water and for communication people used a telephone at the village headman's household. The village relied on solar energy. Connections between Mae Ta La and other localities were therefore difficult. The village social life centred on the river where families gathered for daily baths as well as the washing of clothes, dishes and motorbikes. Children enjoyed snorkelling and playing games in and along the river.

Like in Huay Tong, village space revealed socio-economic and political status differences among villagers. Social differentiation was observable alongside the river, where wealthier and more established households were located upriver. For example, the household of the village headman was located right at the entrance to the village, the most upstream point of the settlement. This location had the privilege and the responsibility of being the first point where visitors were received and where the clearest water for personal care, cooking and laundry could be used. Livelihoods in Mae Ta La were based on swidden agriculture and supplemented by the riches of the flora and fauna around the river. Some of the everyday tasks in Mae Ta La, like rice pounding in the morning, are considered 'archaic' in Huay Tong where few households husk and pound their own rice. In 2008, Mae Ta La village was still rather self-sufficient. Apart from a little grocery store owned by the household of the village head and an even tinier shop, no one ran a business. Nevertheless, there was a growing need for cash income to pay for children's education in government schools.

The Thai administration was marginally represented through the village headman. Otherwise, only the Buddhist *wat* and the state school outside the village served as gentle reminders of the Thai nation state. Until 2001, Buddhist monks who were educated in lowland monasteries provided basic modern education to the children of Mae Ta La. At the time the fieldwork was conducted, the monks were helping by linking adolescent boys with temple schools in lowland towns where the boys became ordained as novices and were enrolled at a secondary school. The absence of modern Thai state institutions and bureaucratic processes impacted on the seemingly 'unorganised' way villagers conceive of bureaucratic issues, such as filling out forms as part of the enrolment procedures for education at Thai state schools. They often asked for assistance in these steps from relatives who were familiar with the working of modern institutions because they work and study in more centralized locations like Huay Tong.

State education was largely absent in Mae Ta La, despite the existence of a school building. There was no kindergarten, and primary education was scarce and of poor quality. The first government school in Mae Ta La was built in 2001, in the wake of the 1997 education policy and the Thai governments' commitment to improve access to formal education in the highlands. Located about 300 metres outside the village, the school was indeed easily accessible. However, few Thai teachers were willing to work in such a remote location. Consequently, the first two years of primary school were taught on a very irregular basis.

During fieldwork in Mae Ta La I shared an evening meal with her host's relatives and neighbours and afterwards embarked on a spontaneous and lengthy discussion on education in the village. At this time, there was one teacher in charge of 35 children. According to villagers, the teacher only taught one week per month. On these occasions, he did not lodge in Mae Ta La but slept in another village. Therefore, parent-teacher contact was scarce and the teacher gave the impression of shunning interaction with Mae Ta La villagers. Moreover, he was said to arrive late in the mornings, and therefore the limited study time was not used well because he apparently preferred to sleep while the children were sent to work on tasks around the school compound. Therefore, Mae Ta La children remained largely illiterate. During our discussion, one young man, who worked as a teaching assistant pointed at the link between villagers' political and economic marginalization, geographic isolation and unequal access to education: 'They say the children here cannot read and write and that they are stupid, but if the teacher does not come, how shall they learn?' In the eyes of Mae Ta La villagers, their limited access to state education also explained their political and economic marginality. However, in an expanding cash economy, they felt the need to connect to the institutions of the modern nation state, such as health clinics and schools. Cash was necessary to cover health bills and school fees as well as gasoline expenses for motorbike journeys. Parents largely relied on their children to provide this income. Therefore, in order to attend state schools, most children migrated for education to live in foster households or governmental dormitories in other villages. Their movements were not unstructured, but were instead supported through foster families and scholarship programmes.

During fieldwork in Huay Tong, I stayed for several months with a local Karen guest family. The warm welcome at the home of Maliwan and her husband was crucial for the success of the research. The family was well connected beyond Mae Wang district to Chiang Mai, Mae Sot and Bangkok. Because of their high social status among the Karen, Maliwan and her husband, as well as their siblings, had many responsibilities to care for those who were less advantaged. Their case study highlights how foster practices help children who move into a household of a higher socioeconomic status in order to access formal education. Maliwan's generous dedication to helping poorer children access education through fosterage and scholarship programmes is related to her siblings: her younger sister-in-law's connections to Mae Ta La and her older brother Vinai Boonule SJ, a Jesuit priest in Chiang Mai. The connection between Maliwan's household in Huay Tong and the children of Mae Ta La village was established by her younger sister and her brother-in-law Hpa Nif, who was the son of the village headman Mae Ta La. Because of her familiarity with the village and especially through the family connection, Maliwan's younger sister was in a position to help aspirational Mae Ta La families who wanted their children to migrate to Huay Tong for their formal education as her sister Maliwan provided a foster home there.

The example of Naw Hpo Muu's migration to Maliwan's foster home household in Huay Tong highlights the interdependencies between intergenerational relations in household economies, modern institutions as well as individual aspirations. Naw Hpo Muu was born in the Mae Ta La village, in the Mae Chaem district. Her mother died when she was three months old, so she was raised in the village by her father and maternal grandmother, as well as an uncle and aunt. Naw Hpo Muu has an older brother who worked in a hotel in Chiang Mai. As a child, Naw Hpo Muu rarely attended school. Instead, she helped her father with agricultural work. The family suffered economic privation when at times there was no rice available and Naw Hpo Muu ate bananas for days. Her father lives in the same village in a house close to her grandmother's house and struggles with alcohol and drug problems. In 2004, Naw Hpo Muu was 12 years old and became the first Mae Ta La child to move to Maliwan's household in Huay Tong village. Her migration for education was made possible by Maliwan's younger sister who, as mentioned previously, was married to the son of Mae Ta La's village headman. When Naw Hpo Muu arrived in Huay Tong, she could not read. She joined Huay Tong School for the last year of primary education and had to catch up on a lot of instruction that the other child had already mastered. She received a government scholarship for her studies in Huay Tong school and lived and worked in her foster household. I met Naw Hpo Muu for the first time in Huay Tong in December 2007. At the time she was 16 years old and was attending the last year of lower secondary school. She was an outstanding student both in grade performance as well as in taking on responsibilities in the school compound. The distance between Mae Ta La Ta village and Huay Tong took around three hours to cover on motorbike. Usually, Naw Hpo Muu only returned to Mae Ta La once a year for the national Songkran festival in April. She missed the feeling of being relaxed at home where she could do whatever she wanted. At the same time, she placed a high value on education: 'Sometimes, I like to go home, I miss home but education is important' (Naw Hpo Muu, 10 August 2009). After graduation from Huay Tong, Naw Hpo Muu attended higher secondary school in the lowlands and then moved to Chiang Mai. When the I met her in 2014, she was attending evening classes at a Buddhist temple school and worked during the week in a Japanese restaurant. During holidays she returned to Mae Ta La where she supported her grandmother with the money she earned in the city.

Scholarship Programmes

Having established the importance of foster families, in this section I shall turn to scholarship programmes that complement the expenses of Karen children's education in Huay Tong. In May 2008, Maliwan and her husband were taking care of 15 foster children: 10 girls and five boys between the age of 10 and 17. The foster children had different origins. Four girls and one boy came from poor villages surrounding Huay Tong and received scholarships for their education from the Jesuit Social Services (JESS) Scholarship Programme. This scholarship programme was open to all deprived children independent of their religious background. Therefore, the scholarship programme is quite innovative, because although Catholic schools in Thailand are famous for their excellent education, only few people, including Catholics, can afford sending their children there (Calderisi 2013: 138). This development of scholarship programmes is also an example of how globalization allows those engaged in religious activities to access transnational networks (Davie 2007: 206). At the time of fieldwork, the Jesuits in Chiang Mai and Bangkok organized fundraising activities in the city and distributed donations through local assistants to children and youth from economically disadvantaged households. The majority of the children who received scholarships were Buddhist, some were Christian and some animist. The programme covered the costs of sheltering children from distant villages in foster households, as well as expenses for uniforms, study materials, school lunches, school fees and the construction of dormitories.

The scholarship programme relied on intergenerational relations within and between foster families. During the time of fieldwork, Maliwan assisted her older brother with the implementation of this scholarship programme. She visited families who were interested in sending their children to Huay Tong for secondary school education. Most of her foster children were related to her. One boy, a nephew of Maliwan's, grew up in the Mae

Hong Son province, while nine of Maliwan's foster children originated from Mae Chaem district, eight of whom were from Mae Ta La, the village of origin of her brother-in-law. Two children from Mae Ta La were close kin of her brother-in-law. All the girls were accommodated within the family compound. The boys spent their nights in a hut on land owned by Maliwan's family behind the school compound. While she cared for her foster children's basic needs, such as food, accommodation and study material, Maliwan also transmitted cultural knowledge like weaving. In fact, she took on responsibilities she believed the foster children's parents did not fulfil and complemented what she perceived as their parents' lack of education. For the bringing up of foster children, Ratana relied on economic support from various sources. Firstly, she received scholarship money for the school expenses of all children in her care. In addition to the scholarship money, she mobilized other sources to cover the expenses of hosting foster children in her house. Some parents contributed with rice and vegetable provisions, but not all were able to do so. So Maliwan made additional efforts to generate household resources. For instance, in February 2008, I accompanied Maliwan, her husband, five foster girls and one boy to harvest cabbage leftovers in a field in the nearby village. The owner of the field sold his produce to the Royal Project, but he allowed others to pick the remains for free. In a short period of time we had gathered five large sacks of cabbages. This was enough to sustain the household for up to two weeks and to have some left to serve up in her seasonal noodle stall business.

While the foster system made it possible for highland children to pursue their educational aspirations, it also allowed Maliwan to increase her socio-economic household aspirations. For household tasks, the foster children worked in separate groups before and after school. The boys helped construct wooden chicken coops or took care of the cattle. Especially during the hot season, they herded cattle beyond the village together with Maliwan's brother-in-law from Mae Ta La. During the long school holidays in the hot season, two foster boys engaged in paid work as gardeners in the Jusuit Seven Fountains retreat centre in Chiang Mai. The boys enjoyed the experience as they earned more than they would have at the Royal Project and had the opportunity to explore the city in their free time.

During the rainy season, all the children's work assistance was particularly important. Maliwan's family owned many rice fields in Huay Tong and the surrounding area. Since most of her family members were professionally active in the lowlands, they relied on others to maintain these fields. If it were not for the foster children, the family would have needed to hire labour to complete the seasonal work on time. Throughout the month of May most households in Huay Tong were busy transplanting rice and towards the end of June weeding had to proceed with urgency. During this time, most children in Huay Tong assisted their families in the paddies. I observed foster children working more than their peers and having less free time to socialize or attend religious ceremonies. With foster children working in the fields, the household and the shop, Maliwan was able to expand her business. In 2014, Maliwan's shop offered the widest range of products in Huay Tong, including sweets and snacks, toiletries and household items.

Of course, the foster system reveals the unequal status between households and villages situated at different geographic locations in northern Thailand. Though foster and biological parents negotiated the treatment of children, they did not negotiate on an equal basis. Foster children and their parents critiqued and contested Maliwan's household. For example, some parents complained to Ratana about the amount of work she demanded from the children in foster care at her home. Such complaints, in turn, upset Maliwan who felt tired because of the huge demands of foster care and of what she felt perceived is the girls' low work ethic. The older girls from Mae Ta La in particular needed constant encouragement to work and study. Maliwan ascribed the children's slow working pace and unreliability to their rural background, saying they arrived in Huay Tong already 'lazy from the village' and that in remote places like Mae Ta La, parents never conferred onerous chores on their daughters and so failed to instil in them a sense of the modern values of duty and economic efficacy. Indeed as outlined above because of the uneven socio-economic development, people in Mae Ta La were not as exposed to the values of modern market economies. The resulting contestations between Maliwan, the foster children and their parents highlighted the importance of geographic location and modes of production in generating diversity in children's upbringing and education. Emerging status differences, in turn, strongly shape local childhood transition experiences.

Children's Agency

During fieldwork the author found Karen children participating to some extent in the regulation of their migration for education. In 2014 access to education was still unequal and depended on children's social status, which, in turn, intersects with their household status or place of residence. Karen children whose households were well connected and familiar with the working of modern Thai institutions and state bureaucracy may have accessed several funding sources. This was highlighted by Darunee's case study, which is expanded on later in this chapter. Her example illustrated political-economic status differences between Karen children growing up in different households and different geographic locations.

For the majority of households in Huay Tong, Maliwan was the first person to ask about scholarships. Indeed Maliwan offered all foster children in her household assistance with identifying high schools and securing funding. Application procedures required a lot of coordination and time resources from Maliwan and her husband. They had to take students to the local administration to copy their ID cards, bring them on assigned days to the schools and help them fill out the application forms. Thai teachers also helped individual students to find places of study in the lowlands. In addition, some students applied through the village priest to missionary schools, like Mae Pon School described in Chap. 2. For instance, during fieldwork, I followed 13-year-old Sedha's transition to Mae Pon School. In early 2008, Sedha had decided to stop attending Huay Tong School and assisted his parents in their grocery store. Because of his young age, his parents felt that Sedha should finish the obligatory period of schooling. Not being comfortable with the national Thai language, the boy wanted to study in his Karen mother tongue. Sedha consulted with the village priest who suggested a year of studies at Mae Pon School. In this way, Sedha was able to take a break from state education and consider with other students and teachers what he could do in the future. Indeed children's peers helped one another to meet persons who help as intermediaries for identifying schools and funding. They relied on shared information as they would not have learned about the opportunity and application procedure from their own parents. As farmers with poor education and limited institutional contacts, their parents were often not equipped to plan their sons' education themselves. In contrast, Maliwan's good command of the Thai and English language, her familiarity with the Thai school system and administration as well as her contacts with the Jesuit Order in Chiang Mai all allowed her to discern opportunities and find ways to follow them up. In this way, Naw Hpo Muu introduced her best friend Panida to Maliwan. Up until her graduation from lower secondary school in Huay Tong, Panida's studies had been supported by a Japanese scholarship. Throughout her last school year Panida thought that she would continue her education in a high school close to Sanpathong and trusted that her older sister would provide the necessary financial support. However, in mid-April it transpired that her family could not support her. Panida worried about not being able to continue her studies, but as she was a close friend of Naw Hpo Muu's, Panida's case became known to Maliwan. Through the Jesuit Social Service scholarship programme, Maliwan asked for modest funding that allowed Panida to attend Santisuk school, a regional welfare school. These Karen foster children of low social status were able to assist each other in finding ways to follow their educational aspirations. This highlighted children's attempts to participate in social change despite their marginalized political-economic status.

Peer Relations as Status Relations

This section highlights the importance of institutional affiliation and geographic location in Karen children's changing peer relations. According to my analysis children's relationships in the village were largely organized according to the socio-economic status of their household. Intergenerational relations and socio-economic status thus structured the relationships among the children in the village. However, Karen children are not only members of household institutions but also of other institutional settings such as state schools. Government schooling has generated new patterns of peer relations among children. Unlike in the village, schools organize boys' and girls' activities according to age-graded batches. So on the school compound children form batch-bounded friendships, and whilst in the village they rely on peer relations. Sanya Kasetsukchai explained: 'In school, when you are from the same batch, you are doing activities together and have more and more relationships. You don't mingle with the other batches at school. Sometimes you don't even have time to talk with the younger ones' (Kasetsukchai, interview, 28 May 2008). In other words, children change their peer relations with one another even as they move within the same village space between the school compound and their households.

The relationship between Naw Hpo Muu, Panida and Darunee illustrates this dynamic of flexible peer relations. As outlined above, Naw Hpo Muu and Panida both grew up in the resource-poor Mae Chaem district and lived as foster children in Huay Tong. Both finished primary school in Mae Chaem and relocated to Huay Tong for secondary education. Naw Hpo Muu lived with Maliwan and her husband, and Panida dwelt in the household of her younger maternal aunt. When they were not at school, both worked with their foster parents for their foster homes' household subsistence. Darunee, in contrast, was born in Huay Tong and was the eldest daughter of the village head. She did not have to work at home and, except for the occasional light household chores, she was free to do her homework and relax. Arguably, there existed considerable difference in the social status of the three girls. Nevertheless, at school they were peers and their status differences were expressed only in very subtle ways. Throughout lower secondary school, the three girls attended the same class and were among the best students who sat in the front row. They were diligent in helping their teachers with practical tasks such as delivering messages, cleaning the library after school, etc. Because of their helpfulness and correctness of manner, their teacher considered them as having a proper demeanour. Neither Naw Hpo Muu's older age nor Darunee's higher socio-economic status rendered their school relations a senior/junior relationship. However, outside school this alliance was not sustainable. In the village, different norms structured peer interaction. While Panida remained Naw Hpo Muu's trusted friend in Huay Tong, Darunee associated mostly with her younger sister and her older female cousins. While in the village, Darunee did not mix with her school peers and made no attempt to conceal her higher social status. For example, on Sundays, she and her village peers regularly visited Maliwan's shop where Naw Hpo Muu worked as a shop assistant. Darunee and her girlfriends usually took a seat on the bench in front of the shop, ordering noodles or ice cream from Naw Hpo Muu who also served them. I observed Naw Hpo Muu, in turn, using strategies not to lose face because of her lower socio-economic status. Once, after Darunee left, Naw Hpo Muu remarked that she did not like the particular ice cream her schoolmate had just bought. Claiming that the ice cream had no personal value for her, Naw Hpo Muu expressed her indifference with regard to the product desired and consumed by Darunee. In this way, Naw Hpo Muu saved face concerning her inability to spend money. Importantly, she was doing so in assuming a position of 'indifference'. Therefore, from a Buddhist point of view, in keeping a detached and 'cool' demeanour, Naw Hpo Muu positioned herself in a morally higher position than Darunee who was excited by the ice cream and the desire to consume it. Despite their unequal socio-economic and political status in Huay Tong, the three girls have all been able to make the transition to high school in Ban Kad. This is possible because all three accessed funding high school programmes.

In May 2008, Darunee and Naw Hpo Muu moved with other girls for high school to Ban Kad high school. Weekly commutes between Huay Tong and Ban Kad impacted on the status differences among peers. In the lowlands, vis-à-vis others, Huay Tong high school students constituted themselves as a group that shared a common place of residence, i.e. Huay Tong village. The shared high school experience in Ban Kad impacted on Naw Hpo Muu and Darunee's friendship. In the lowlands, Naw Hpo Muu's identity and status were not primarily defined by her being a foster child belonging to an impoverished household from a remote village. Instead, she belonged to the peer group who arrived from the mountain village Huay Tong in the lowland town Ban Kad. Accordingly, she shared study and working activities at school *and* outside school with her peers from the village, including Darunee. They all lodged in the same dormitory run and sponsored by the Jesuit Order. Moreover, they used the same school room and bedroom and ate out of the same rice pot. Indeed at the time of fieldwork, high school students in northern Thailand formed groups according to their villages, and within these groups they were organized according to seniority. Importantly, the place of reference was not their village of birth, but rather the village they 'come from' to study in Ban Kad. This is why it was possible for Naw Hpo Muu and Darunee to be in the same group 'coming from Huay Tong' each week and returning there for the weekend. The organization of daily dormitory and school life mirrored the importance of geographic location. Although there were Karen students from other places lodging in the dormitory, the girls from Huay Tong rarely mixed with them. The sitting order during evening meals, as well as the distribution of sleeping places, was arranged according to groups from similar geographic areas. Chores were also organized according to these group patterns. Usually, groups performed tasks in alternation, for example one week the Huay Tong group was responsible for cooking breakfast and the next week for sweeping the floors. Naw Hpo Muu contrasted the rigid division of chores at her foster household with the task rotation at the dormitory: 'here it is not like in Huay Tong'. She enjoyed the new liberty of relaxing after school, for example, playing volleyball with her peers at the dormitory. She emphasized that everyone at the dormitory gathered for shared evening meals and contrasted this with the segregated food consumption in the foster home. Throughout the school day, the girls from Huay Tong remained in their peer group and had only minimal contact with students of other ethnic groups, such as the Hmong and lowland Thais. Speaking about her social relations with students from other locations, Naw Hpo Muu described Hmong students as 'friendly': 'We can play together'. In contrast, lowland Thai students seemed less trustworthy to her: 'I don't know, but we do not like each other', because they bullied and thought they are better than 'people from the mountains'. Remaining largely within the same group provided a sense of security and reduced the risk of being bullied. One teacher at Ban Kad school confirmed that Karen and Hmong girls tended to go through the school day in groups with peers of the same ethnicity. They rarely mixed with local Thai students in the classrooms, canteen or school yard when resting. Staying among peers also allowed them to speak in their mother tongue. For instance, during difficult classroom exercises, students consulted one another in their own language. It was important to note that Thai teachers talked about 'ethnic' groups without reference to intra-Karen differences that were defined according to geographic location and political-economic status. However, the Huay Tong girls' weekday solidarity did not extend to weekends. On Fridays, the girls returned in the late afternoon or early evening to the village. Upon their return, they resumed their village roles and responsibilities according to the political-economic status of their households; so their weekend experiences differed accordingly. For example, Darunee and other girls, whose households were of higher status in Huay Tong, stayed at home most of the weekends. When asked about their weekend activities, they typically said: 'I am at home. Resting'. However, this did not mean that they were literally resting all weekend. Instead, they did leisurely work, such as feeding pigs and helping their mothers sell gasoline while studying and chatting with others. In contrast, Naw Hpo Muu's high school attendance did not mitigate her weekend working obligations in Maliwan's foster home. From Friday evening until late afternoon on Sunday, she worked in Maliwan's shop. In fact, Naw Hpo Muu's weekend presence allowed Maliwan and her family to engage in social activities, attend Mass and leave Huay Tong for business or family affairs in Chiang Mai. Naw Hpo Muu confided to her Mae Ta La peers that she was tired and tense because of her tough studies and the huge amounts of daily homework. At the same time, however, her new role as a high school student in Ban Kad enhanced her senior status among the other foster children who still attended Huay Tong School. She signalled her new status by making little comments and bringing gifts such as a hairband from Ban Kad market for her junior friends. Therefore, commuting between the highlands and lowlands children assumed different social status at different locations. My data on changing peer relations highlighted the children's ability to become increasingly flexible in positioning themselves socially in different locations.

Karen students' migration for education impacts on gender relations and social morality. During fieldwork in Thailand, I found that morality standards among the Karen depend on the geographic location of villages. The range of permissible sociability between boys and girls differed throughout the highlands. I found Karen high school girls seriously concerned over complying with moral standards and being careful not to disappoint their families. Indeed according to a worksheet-based survey, the fear of 'not being a good daughter' was a major reason for 'feeling bad' among girls. For them, it was undesirable to be known as a rebellious character or 'not so good person'. Instead, girls who were smart convinced others in public of their 'good behaviour'. Moral reputation was also linked to the peers with whom the girls kept company. Girls who appeared in public with the same gender or kin peers had the reputation of being a 'good person'. By contrast, gossip about 'bad' friendships or romantic relations could ruin reputations, so girls often concealed their feelings. For example, Karen high school girls made an effort to manage their emotional expressions in front of adults and their peers. In the lowlands, they needed to ensure their lives were accountable to their home communities, lest they became subjects of gossip. Indeed stories of young women returning pregnant to the mountains did circulate. The common explanation was that in the city 'they are lonely', i.e. detached from their household and village community. Therefore, Karen girls who migrated for education to lowland towns often chose accommodation in reputable dormitories where they felt their good reputation would not be harmed. Moralities around boys' and girls' friendship patterns also differed according to geographic location and institutional affiliation. For teenage girls from Huay Tong, the Ban Kad dormitory run by the Jesuit Order provided a reputable abode during their high school studies.

Gendered patterns of mobility for young people change depending on where they are located. In general, Karen teenage girls' mobility seems more restricted than that of the boys. At the time of fieldwork, Karen male youth were free to roam the mountains and lowland plains on their motorbikes, while girls' mobility declined as they move towards womanhood.

However, changing locations had an impact on girls' mobility. Although girls may comply with household norms in the village, once they change location and institutional attachment, they are also eager to be mobile. My data reveal that among Karen high school students in Ban Kad, strolling around features among the most popular leisure activities and the ability to 'go where I like' was an important source of happiness. Indeed during my visits to Ban Kad, girls also used motorbikes to travel from the dormitory to the market. They did not travel long distances like their male peers, but they did use motorbikes on excursions.

The appearance of young people also changes as they migrate. In high school in the lowlands, there was more liberty for girls to try out different beauty products and styles. During lunch breaks, girls entertained themselves by using facial powder and experimenting with friends' hairstyles. Male classmates joined them, playing with their gendered identities in putting on mascara and lipstick. This would not have been easily allowed in the village. Thus, studying in the lowlands improved girls' ability to experiment with gendered moralities linked to the social values of highland villages. During their weekend visits to Huay Tong, they flexibly re-adapted their behaviour to local morals to ensure their 'good' reputation remained unsullied. Therefore, their overall agency in challenging gendered patterns of normative behaviour remained constrained and needed to be understood in relation to compliance of norms and values.

Sociocultural Identities

As outlined above, geographic locations can enhance or mitigate socio-economic and political inequalities among Karen children, as well as between them and lowland Thai children. During fieldwork, I found Karen children expressed social distance or belonging to places by employing locally valued cultural symbols. Socio-economic inequality was more acutely felt in the lowlands than in the villages. Despite socio-economic diversity among the children, high school students insisted that the organization of daily livelihood provisions and social relations at school were easier in highland villages than in the lowland towns because, for example, fellow villagers were not 'serious about time'. In contrast, in mainstream society, Karen girls felt they 'have to think hard' to organize their daily livelihoods. Living expenses were indeed lower in the mountains where there was no need to pay rent; food was either grown in private gardens or gathered from around the village, and potable water was freely available at the village well. This was partly why people said they preferred living there and value that location over the lowlands.

Subjective feelings also indicated distance and belonging to locations. Social distance seemed to increase as children migrated to bigger places.

For instance, foster children from Mae Ta La mentioned that in their heart they missed their native village. Although Mae Ta La was much poorer than Huay Tong, in the eyes of Naw Hpo Muu and other children it was more 'fun', 'because it is our home'. In contrast to Huay Tong, they felt that in their home village they could make themselves comfortable and do as they pleased. Children from Huay Tong, in turn, felt marginalized when they visited lowland towns, detached from their household institutions in the highland village. Naw Hpo Muu said that in Huay Tong 'everyone is friendly'; in contrast, in Ban Kad people who knew each other from school but often did not greet each other outside the parameters of the school compound. Social distance was felt even more intensively in 'the city'. In Chiang Mai, for instance, neighbours were said to live next to each other without making any contact. During a chat at the village well, a 12-year-old girl explained: 'Chiang Mai is hot, there is no happiness'. In contrast, the highlands are described as having a 'pleasant and better atmosphere'. Obviously, the weather is used here to describe general feelings: whilst the hot weather symbolizes tension and stress, the 'pleasant and better atmosphere' refers to a situation where people feel relaxed and at ease. She further explained that in the lowlands, 'you are not with your parents and start missing them', emphasizing her argument by making a gesture of a tender embrace in the air.

The use of cultural symbols can be a strategic means to emphasize belonging or distance to a place. Indeed during fieldwork, I found that between poor and resource-rich Karen highland villages, the symbolic value of products changed according to location. Therefore, a product considered valuable in one place can become a sign of poverty and a cause of shame in a different location. For example, in Mae Ta La, sugar cubes and tea are popular snacks. Naw Hpo Muu enjoyed consuming these snacks with peers and relatives during her home visit to Mae Ta La. However, when she was in Huay Tong, Naw Hpo Muu ceased to eat sugar cubes or drink tea. This was because in Huay Tong manufactured sweets and juices could be bought in shops, and sugar cubes were sold as the cheapest sweets; Naw Hpo Muu knew that for villagers in Huay Tong, sugar cubes and sweets were associated with their past childhoods and poverty. Moreover, between the highlands and the lowlands, Karen children and youth shifted strategically between their Thai and Karen names. When they moved to lowland towns for high school, they made increasing use of their Thai names. I assumed that girls and boys might be unhappy at not being able to use their Karen name in the plains. However, my survey revealed that girls were much more relaxed about the issue than I had thought. School girls emphasized their initiative in choosing to use Karen or Thai names, depending on the local context. For example, it was possible to use Karen names in official documents, but out of consideration to Thai officials they used their Thai names as these sounded familiar to Thai people. Otherwise Karen girls worried that 'if it is the Karen name, some people cannot translate it'. Asked about her feelings in shifting between names, Darunee explained: 'I do not feel anything. It's normal. Another girl said she enjoyed the liberty of having many names, and switching between names between the highlands and lowlands protected her from unpleasant visitors. If a Karen person she did not like came to Ban Kad looking for her but only knew her Karen name, they were unable to find her. Among ethnic minorities in Burma and Thailand, clothes are general markers of socio-economic and political status (Dell and Dudley 2003). Also among the Karen, homespun clothes are conventional markers of gender, generational and marital status. During fieldwork in northern Thailand, I found that the Karen largely used clothes to highlight or conceal their Karen ethnic identity. Often, the use of clothes depended on geographic location and their range of interaction with lowland Thai people. For example, in remote areas of Mae Chaem district, such as Mae Ta La village, young people wore their traditional clothes daily. By contrast, in Huay Tong, since the 1980s industrially manufactured clothes have increasingly replaced traditional garments. During fieldwork, the author saw village girls only wearing their *hsei wa* (white dress) and boys their *hsei gauz* (red shirt) for religious feasts, during Sunday Mass and on Fridays at school. As visual symbols of local belonging, homespun clothes also related to socio-economic and political inequalities. For instance, wearing homespun clothes could render children as well as adults vulnerable to discrimination. Accordingly, Karen people avoided wearing homespun garments in the lowlands. Indeed during her fieldwork, I only observed highlanders of very low socio-economic status wearing their traditional clothes at the market or in hospitals around Chiang Mai. Usually, those who could afford it wore clothes purchased in the lowlands. Those who had the financial means might even purchase clothes that were popular in enhancing their 'Thai-ness'. For example, at the time of fieldwork, the yellow Thai shirt, in particular, served as a powerful symbol of loyalty to the Thai royalty and nation. On a weekly basis, each Monday all over Thailand, civil servants, including school teachers, wore yellow shirts. The yellow T-shirts were available in every market in the lowlands, which was also where Karen women obtained these status symbols. In particular, Karen women changed into their yellow T-shirts when they were about to make a visit to the lowlands. Significantly, teenagers often received their first Thai T-shirt when they made their transition to high school in the plains. Signifying belonging to a geographic location was therefore not only an expression of subjective feelings, but also a way to negotiate political and ethnic belonging. Cultural heritage, like the use of mother tongue or the wearing of traditional clothes, can be a means to encourage children's identity. At the same time, ethnic minority children, like the Karen, sometimes prefer to adapt to the majority culture around them. This is particularly important for children who cross international borders and live as refugees and migrants outside their countries of origin. The next chapter turns to this topic.

Bibliography

Ansell, N., and L. van Blerk. 2007. Doing and belonging: Toward a more than-representational account of young migrant identities in Lesotho and Malawi. In *Global perspectives on rural childhood and youth*, ed. R. Panelli, S. Punch, and E. Robson, 17–28. New York: Routledge.

Beale Spencer, M., and C. Markstrom-Adams. 1990. Identity processes among racial and ethnic minority children in America. *Child Development* 61(2): 290–310.

Boyden, J., and G. Crivello. 2014. Childwork and mobility. In *Migration: A compas anthology*, ed. B. Anderson and M. Keith, 37–38. Oxford: COMPAS.

Buadaeng, K. 2005. Thailand: Urban migration and hill tribe youth in Chiang Mai. *Indigenous Affairs* 3: 359–384.

Bushin, N., et al. 2007. Reflecting on contexts and identities for young rural lives. In *Global perspectives on rural childhood and youth*, ed. R. Panelli, S. Punch, and R. Robson, 69–80. New York: Routledge.

Calderisi, R. 2013. *Earthly mission. The Catholic Church and world development.* New Haven: Yale University Press.

Chatty, D. 2010. *Displacement and dispossession in the modern Middle East.* Cambridge: Cambridge University Press.

Crivello, G. 2009. *'Becoming somebody': Youth transitions through education and migration—Evidence from Young Lives, Peru.* Oxford: Young Lives. Working Paper No. 43.

Davie, G. 2007. *The sociology of religion.* Los Angeles: Sage Publications.

Dell, E., and S. Dudley (eds.). 2003. *Textiles from Burma. Featuring the James Henry Green Collection.* London: Philip Wilson Publisher.

Elliot, D. 1978. The socio-economic formation of modern Thailand. *Journal of Contemporary Asia* 8(1): 21–50.

Froerer, P. 2011. Education, inequality and social mobility in central India. *European Journal of Development Research* 23: 695–711.

Heissler, K. 2011. 'We are poor people so what is the use of education?' Tensions and contradictions in girls' and boys' transitions from school to work in rural Bangladesh. *European Journal of Development Research* 23: 729–744.

Hinton, E. 1999. *Oldest brother's story: Tales of the Pwo Karen.* Chiang Mai: Silkworm Books.

Holloway, S., and G. Valentine (eds.). 2000. *Children's geographies: Playing, living, learning.* London: Routledge.

Huijsmans, R. 2013. 'Doing gendered age': Older mothers and migrant daughters negotiating care work in rural Lao PDR and Thailand. *Third World Quarterly* 34(10): 1896–1910.

Kasetsukchai, S. 2008. Interview, 28 May 2008.

Kunstadter, P. 1979. Ethnic group, category, and identity: Karen in northern Thailand. In *Ethnic adaptation and identity: The Karen on the Thai frontier with Burma*, ed. C. Keyes, 119–163. Philadelphia: Institute of Human Issues.

Leinaweaver, J. 2008. *The circulation of children: Kinship, adoption, and morality in Andean Peru.* Durham: Durham University Press.

Mischung, R. 1984. *Religion und Wirklichkeitsvorstellungen in einem Karen-Dorf Nordwest-Thailands.* Wiesbaden: Franz Steiner Verlag.

Naw Hpo Muu. 2009. Interview, 10 August 2009.

Nayak, A. 2003. *Race, place and globalization: Youth cultures in a changing world.* Oxford: Berg.

Ni Laoire, C. 2008. Complicating host-newcomer dualisms: Irish return migrants as home-comers or newcomers? *Translocations: Migration and Social Change* 4(1): 35–50.

Panelli, R., S. Punch, and E. Robson (eds.). 2010. *Global perspectives on rural childhood and youth.* New York: Routledge.

Schildkrout, E. 1978. Age and gender in Hausa society: Socio-economic roles of children in urban Kano. In *Sex and age as principles of social differentiation*, ed. J.S. La Fontaine, 109–137. London: Academic Press.

Sheba, G. 2005. *When Women Come First. Gender and Class in Transnational Migration.* Berkeley: University of California Press.

Walker, A. 2001. The 'Karen consensus', ethnic politics and resource-use legitimacy in Northern Thailand. *Asian Ethnicity* 2(2): 145–162.

Wright, E. 2016. Intergenerational Transfers Over the Life Course: Addressing Temporal and Gendered Complexities Via a Human Wellbeing Approach. *Progress in Development Studies*, 16(3) doi:10.1177/1464993416641582.

CHAPTER 6

Education and Displacement at the Thai-Burma Border

Having outlined the value of education in the forms of socio-cultural learning and schooling among the Karen in Burma and Thailand, this chapter turns to education in the context of the displacement of the Karen of Burma. During Burma's 60-year-long armed conflict, the national education system was frequently used to disseminate ideologies of ethno-nationalism hence increasing marginalization of the Karen and other non-Burmese communities (Sadan 2014: 70). Moreover, where Burma's ethnic minorities live in refugee camps in Thailand, new forms of inequality between and among the refugee population, Thai government authorities and international humanitarian aid agencies were created, for example when it came to the questions of how to design culturally sensitive but internationally meaningful curricula for camp-based schools (Metro 2014: 169; Oh 2012: 96). In spite of this evidence, there is little education funding in conflict-affected countries. At the time of writing this book, there was still an urgent need to increase the efficiency of humanitarian aid for education, especially in areas of prolonged crises (Takyi-Amoako 2015: 4–5; UNESCO 2015). In post-conflict settings, too, youth's aspirations for secondary and post-secondary education are frequently neglected, especially among refugees and other exiled persons (Buckland 2006: 8).

The humanitarian situation at the Thailand-Burma border is one of the longest protracted refugee situations in the world. Between 1960 and 1984 Karen villagers have crossed the border with Thailand sporadically. However, in 1984 the Burmese Army launched a massive offensive

P. Jolliffe, *Learning, Migration and Intergenerational Relations*,
DOI 10.1057/978-1-137-57218-9_6

and succeeded in breaking through the Karen front lines opposite the Tak Province. As a consequence, about 10,000 Karen refugees arrived in Thailand (Rogers 2004: 157). During the following ten years, until 1994, the Burmese Army continued launching attacks and more people decided to cross the Thai border, reaching about 80,000 in 1994.Two other key moments concerning the displacement of persons across the Thai-Burma border have been the 1988 and 1990 Democracy Movements. In 1988 monks and students rose against the military regime with Aung San Suu Kyi as their inspiration. After the crackdown of the movement around 10,000 student activists sought shelter in Thailand. It was in this context that for the first time alliances between the ethnic and pro-democracy movements were initiated. In 1990 the State Law and Order Restoration Council (SLORC) initiated General Elections that were won by Aung San Suu Kyi's National League for Democracy (NLD). However, the party was not allowed to take power and a campaign of imprisonment and intimidation of elected Members of Parliament was initiated. Since the dissolution of the military junta in 2011, a process of transitioning towards democracy was initiated by the government which was still largely led by military officials. Within Burmese post-conflict society, the context of education remained strongly politicized (British Council 2014: 4). For example, in 2014 official school textbooks still had few references to the ethnic, religious and linguistic minority groups (Traedwell 2014: 56).

Lack of Education in Rural Burma

As outlined in Chap. 3, the Karen in Burma enrolled in missionary schools throughout the nineteenth and early twentieth centuries. However, their access to formal education decreased considerably during the decades of armed conflict. Following the 1962 military coup, all schools in Burma were nationalized. As a consequence, by 1966 all foreign Christian missionaries directly in charge of schools were expelled from the country. Public schools, like the prestigious Methodist English High School in Rangoon, were transformed into state schools, and Burmese became the medium of instruction without consideration of ethnic minority vernacular languages (Thein Lwin 2003: 59). This development particularly affected poor people in rural areas who spoke a different mother tongue than Burmese. For example, Sister Eugenie is a Pwo karen who was born in 1959 and grew up in Chanthagone, Irrawaddy Delta. In an interview she remembered that education was highly valued in her family and home community. Her grandfather was a school teacher and headmaster. Likewise, her father became headmaster of the village school. The school in Eugenie's village was so good that Burmese children from the surrounding villages migrated for education at her village school. Nevertheless, children's access to education depended on their social status. Not every family was able to pay school fees, textbook and stationery, and Sister Eugenie estimated that half of the children in her village never attended school and remained illiterate. Even those children who attended government school only learned how to read and write in the national Burmese language. Their Pwo Karen mother tongue was not part of the school curriculum. Boys and girls had, however, the opportunity to study with Karen priests and nuns who privately taught how to read and write Pwo Karen. Typically, these tuitions took place outside school at boarder houses (Sister Eugenie, interview, 8 March 2015). Buddhist monks, too, provided education for Karen children. In this respect, Daw Aung San Suu Kyi described in her famous *Letters from Burma* (1996) her visit to the Buddhist middle school and elementary school at Wekayin village in Hpa-an township of Karen State:

'It is a big rickety wooden building on stilts and the whole school assembled on the beaten earth floor between the stilts to pay their respects to the *Hsayadaw*[1], who distributed roasted beans to everybody. The 375 children are taught by thirteen teachers struggling with a dearth of equipment. The headmaster is a young man with an engaging directness of manner who talked, without the slightest trace of self-pity or discouragement, about the difficulties of acquiring even such basic materials as textbooks. Of course the situation of Wekayin middle school is no different from that of schools all over Burma but it seemed especially deserving of assistance because of the dedication of the teachers and the happy family atmosphere' (Aung San Suu Kyi 1996: 16). On the way to the elementary school, the group picked up some children who seemed particularly cheerful. Daw Aung San Suu Kyi's observations are important because they highlight two seemingly contrasting phenomenon: first, the extreme destitution of the mid-1990s school educational system in Burma and second the happiness and joy of teachers and students who attended these schools. A similar portrait of students' happiness in poor schools emerged from the essays a group of Karen refugee students wrote on 25 March 2015. In their essays, Karen girls and boys in their early twenties reflect on the role of school in their lives. They described how their primary schools in Burma were only built out of bamboo. There was a lack of study material such as pens, books and stationery. Although their teachers were

Karen, the medium of instruction was Burmese and students found it difficult to study in a language that was not their own mother tongue. And yet, there were also memories of happiness and gratitude for the education received. For example, Poe Thay, a young Karen refugee in Chiang Mai wrote in an essay:

> 'When I was a child I studied in primary school. My school was built by bamboo and the roof was made by leaves. My school was not rich in material like, pencil, pen, books, chalk. So we had to face many troubles in this school. My teachers were not successful in their teaching skill so we didn't know a lot how to read and write. (...) In 1999, I went to another village. So, I saw a new school which was better than where I had studied before. I know my skills became better because of high school but I never forget the school where I had studied before.' (Poe Thay, essay, 25 March 2015)

Because of the unstable situation in rural Burma, the beginning schooling was sometimes delayed. For instance, one research participant was already 12-years old when he started attending school:

> 'When I was a child my parents loved me and talked to me about education. I listened to my parents but, I was so lazy to go to school to get education in my life. When I was 12 years old I started to go to school on 20th August. The school location was in Toe Wee Der village. I lived together with my grand mom near the school. My school started at 8 am and finished at 3 pm. After I had finished school I went back home where I helped my grandmother with cooking and carrying water.' (Eh Htee, essay, 25 March 2015)

Dropout rates were high throughout the country. The reasons for children dropping out of school are numerous. For example, child-related factors included illness and lack of interest. In other cases, families were unable to cover school expenses or needed their child to assist with chores at home for the household economy. There were also factors related to the school itself such as distance between school and children's home, lack of teachers, teaching materials and dormitories (Thein Lwin 2003: 64–65).

Displacement, too, can be a reason for dropping out of school. During her fieldwork with Burmese refugee youth, I found that the war and fighting caused frequent displacement of children and their families. Because of this internal displacement, students frequently had to interrupt their primary school education and move to another village where they adapted to another school. High school students had to drop out when their families were unable or unwilling to further support their children's schooling. For example, Moebue, born in 1986, recalled how she had to drop out of school after the death of her mother:

> 'Until 1995 the memories of going to school were peaceful. But in 1996, when I was in grade 5 and 6, we had a lot of fighting going. We have hardly been to any school but then passed the exams somehow. And my mother decided to send me to Pruso township in Karenni State, for better education and a better standard for living. And also there was a long fighting going on in the village and so she sent me to Pruso. We had to pay the school fees and books, everything. And I went to Pruso for three years. And in the second year, when I was in grade eight, my mother passed away. After my mother passed away it was really hard for me to continue my education because my father doesn't know how to read and write; he is not educated. He is not a particular person who encourages you to study and tell you to go to school. It is difficult because he had no idea. My mother went to school and knew how to read and write. And this is very different. (...) I studied there for three years and then after grade 10 I went to Loikow for boarding school. I went there for one year. I did not complete my studies in this year because my father could not keep me longer in school and I had to return home. Costs included not only the school fees, but also electricity and rice. Everything was costly and he could not afford that. So, I had to go home and stay with my father. And then the Burmese Army came to our village and fought and my father was really worried. I was 15. My brothers were also at home. They did not continue with school because we had no money. So, my father sent me to the refugee camps' (Moebue, interview, 23 June 2015).

Moebue's example highlights the importance of parents' education. Indeed whether or not parents value education often corresponds to the education they received: Moebue's mother was literate and interested in her daughter's school education. When school attendance in the village became dangerous because of armed conflict, Moebue's mother sent her daughter to Pruso where she lodged with an uncle and attended school. In addition to securing the material needs of her daughter, Moebue's mother also seems to have been an important moral support in encouraging Moebue to focus on her school education. At this point she says, the death of her mother had an immediate impact on her studies. Her illiterate father was unable to encourage Moebue in a similar way as her mother—who was literate and valued formal education—did. Nevertheless, Moebue's father allowed his daughter to go to high school in Loikow until he was no longer able to pay for study expenses. In this way Moebue had to drop out of school.

The impoverishment of her family coincided with political instability as the fighting increased. In the light of these political and economic constraints, Moebue's father worried about his daughter's safety and eventually sent her to seek refuge in Thailand. Moebue's own journey took her three months through the jungle. She left her family home in October 2002 and arrived in New Year 2003 in a refugee camp in Thailand.

Post-secondary Education in Refugee Camps

When Moebue arrived in the camp she resumed her studies and completed grade 10 in the camp's high school. Like Moebue, thousands of ethnic minority youth had to interrupt their schooling in Burma. However, displacement and flight to Thailand did not extinguish young peoples' thirst for education. Once they arrived in Thai refugee camps many resumed their studies. In August 2014, The Border Consortium still counted a camp population of 120,174 persons. More than half of this population—63,009 persons—were under the age of 18. Indeed over the last 20 years a whole generation of young people was born in and around refugees camps and grew up in exile without much contact with their parents' or grandparents' places of origin (Group interview, 30 May 2015). These young people aspire to access high school and post-secondary education. Bridget Robinson, a Maltese teacher at the Thailand-Burma border remembers: 'The students used to travel on their own, particularly for education. Many of the young were unaccompanied. They didn't have parents to turn to. They would come at every age starting from 11 or 12, especially in the mid-teens. They came in search for education. So, although there were some families in the camp, the predominant structure of the camp were youth in search of education' (Bridget Robinson, interview, 13 March 2015). Unaccompanied children typically found accommodation in boarding houses in the camps, where a range of community-based organizations, non-governmental organizations and international organizations promoted education, such as Jesuit Refugee Service (JRS), Women`s Education for Advancement and Empowerment (WEAVE), and ZOA Refugee Care. Bridget Robinson also mentioned that the existence of boarding houses for unaccompanied students was not without controversy for they were perceived to act as a pull factor encouraging students to come to the camps, but at the same time they provided a disciplined structure which helped with the smooth running of the camps.

Of course, the relations between humanitarian aid organizations, Thai authorities and Burmese refugees speak of unequal power configuration along socio-cultural and political-economic lines. Indeed the governance of Burmese refugee camps in Thailand was complex. It involved state authorities, humanitarian agencies as well as armed non-state actors who, in disguised or overt ways, competed with each other regarding the authority over camp sites and the people residing therein (Vogler 2007: 53). Rose Metro's research highlights educational challenges in camps at the Thailand-Burma border. First, she identified competing agenda of competing groups within the community and international NGOs cooperation with those refugee groups which had the largest numbers. For example, by promoting the majority Karen language as a medium of instruction, the languages of other minority ethnic groups within the largely Karen refugee camps were ignored. Another challenge was the negotiation between NGOs and the Royal Thai Government, which permitted refugees to run their own schools within the confines of the camp but found it difficult to open up educational pathways outside camps (Metro 2014: 169; Oh 2012: 99). Whilst bearing in mind the structural constraints of camp-based education, the remaining part of this chapter discusses examples of international educational projects which refugee youth themselves perceived as enabling and empowering.

Post Ten School

Post Ten schools were the first schools to offer post-secondary education to Burmese refugee youth in Thailand. The idea of creating Post Ten schools responded to camp youths' increasing demand for education beyond the level of 10th grade in high school. The first Post Ten School was founded in 1995 in Mae Surin Refugee camp, where the majority of camp population were ethnic Karenni, a group closely related to the Karen. As refugees from Burma they were until 2005 not allowed to access education outside the camps. Therefore, the creation of Post Ten schools responded to refugee students' aspiration beyond 10th grade of high school.

Ka Law Lah was among the international team[2] that founded the first Post Ten School. As an educated Karen from Rangoon he worked as an engineer for the Burmese government in Karenni State. Through this work he witnessed many human rights violations and eventually decided to quit his job and join the resistance army. He thus arrived in Thailand where he found work as a teacher in a refugee camp. He lived in refugee camps for about 18 years and throughout his stay there, he served the community as high school principal, Post Ten teacher and education department director. In 1994, the rest of the family followed Ka Law Lah to the Thai side of the Thai-Burma border. His son Mie Tha Lah was 17 years old and had finished his high school in Burma. Thanks to his father, he immediately found work as a teacher in the camp. Mie Tha Lah's sister Wah Paw Lah was 14 and finished her last year of high school in the camp. Wah Paw Lah rememberd the transition to the camp in Thailand. Having grown up in Rangoon, she had a different childhood experience from most of the children who grew up in rural conflict-zone refugee camps. In an interview she explained in broken English: 'I was fourteen years and at that time I was 8 standard. I came here and I cannot mingle with my peer group. They don't talk to me. And I was daunted and asked myself "Why do they don't want to talk to me?" And then, I don't know, they, the camp children those who are grown up inside the camp who are born outside of Burma, they are very straight to the point, they don't pretend. If they don't like, they just show that they don't like. For us, we just pretend, or sometimes we don't like a people, but it is rude to behave so We try to do conversation with them. But for them, if they don't want to talk, they just don't talk' (Wah Paw Lah, interview, 2 February 2006). I met Wah Paw Lah and Mie Tha Lah in early 2006 when she volunteered with the NGO WEAVE (Women's Education for Advancement and Empowerment) on the development of a curriculum project for refugee women. At that time, Wah Paw Lah and Mie Tha Lah were both teachers at a camp Post Ten School. Before that, Mie Tha Lah studied education in the Philippines between 1999 and 2003. Thanks to his high level of education, Mie Tha Lah developed thorough knowledge about different teaching methods. Upon his return to Thailand it was however difficult to communicate his enthusiasm to the students and teachers in the camp. The introduction of a systematic grading system turned into a major challenge. The students in the camp were used to a teacher-centred learning method and their academic performance was based on the final exam alone. So they studied very hard just to pass the final exam. This system seemed rather unfair to the overall academic success of individual students. By contrast, the grading system Mie Tha Lah introduced after his return from the Philippines was based on the categories: Attendance: 10 %, quizzes: 15 %, assignments: 20 %, projects (group work, participation, research, etc.): 25 %, and exams: 30 %. The idea was to score the academic performance based on these areas throughout the year. Mie Tha Lah remembers: We revolutionized the school's grading system, but many of our students did not grasp the logic behind our system for the first two years. However, things gradually worked out in the end' (Mie Tha Lah, email, 29 June 2015).

Bridget Robinson also remembers from a teacher's perspective the difficulties of engaging with deeply ingrained habits of teaching and learning in the refugee camps. Whilst in the West, education aims at encouraging students to discover for themselves to look at the evidence and to come to their own conclusion, the teaching within the politically restricted context of Burma and the refugee camps was usually centred on rote learning. Western teachers sensed that unless students were taught in this way they didn't consider they were being taught properly. All input was expected to come from the teacher, with the students as passive receivers. Lessons often consisted of students reading aloud in turn or the teacher writing on the blackboard for the students to copy. Teachers were also translating word for word out of old English or Burmese textbooks and in doing so the meaning was lost. Often it seemed to Western observers that the point the textbook author was making was entirely missed and one wondered how much of a lesson students had understood or retained. Language, too, was a crucial issue. For example, in the Karenni camps in Mae Hong Son, students of different ethnic background had to learn Karenni for political reasons related to ethno-nationalism. Instead of unifying and teaching all of them Burmese for when they went back, they had to learn Karenni and learn a script that was invented in the camp. It was not used in Kayah State at all, but was just a camp script without use to them anywhere else. Also the education certificates students received from the camp were only recognized within the camp, not anywhere else in the world (Robinson, interview, 13 March 2015).

In order to help students make the transition to learning institutions outside camps, The Curriculum Project, a programme based in Mae Sot, endeavoured to unify the Post Ten syllabi of all the nine camps along the Thailand-Burma border and to teach students Community Development, Social Studies, Environmental Studies, English language modules as well as History from an ethnic minority perspective. This was not always a straightforward process, but it touched upon existing hierarchies between ethnic minority students, their teachers and community elders (Metro 2013: 163). Also, certain subjects, like science, were practically not covered, because the camps did not have the equipment for experiments.

Education speaks about social status. For example, school drop out in the camp was linked to social status. Poor rather than wealthy children dropped out of school to support their household economies (Oh et al.

2010: 58). Moreover, dropout rates spoke about gender inequality since girls who became pregnant were excluded from school, whilst boys who became fathers were allowed to continue their education. Becoming a teacher was a way to gain social status and to return the gift of education to a younger generation of refugee students. Therefore, often immediately after graduation from Post Ten School, many youth became teachers themselves. Therefore, camp teachers were typically very young and knew their students from the time they had been students themselves. This led to problems of discipline because on the one hand, students were expected to respect their teacher for being the teacher, whilst on the other hand they found it difficult to see a former pupil in this respected role. For their initiation into teaching students usually attended a basic teacher training course after graduation from the camp school. Ideally, the training should have lasted one year, but sometimes young people were thrown in as teachers after only one week of training. Bridget Robinson who had experience in teacher training, felt the training in the camps did not have lasting results because those who attended the courses reverted to what was familiar from their own experience. For example, the system of rote learning was not easily replaced by alternative methods of teaching different skills and ideas to develop critical thinking. Soon after her arrival in Mae Hong Son, Bridget's teaching methods resulted in a contretemps with a local teacher who insisted lessons should take the form of a declaration: 'Today we are learning the Past Continuous, followed by a rule and some gap fill exercises' rather than getting the students to use a grammatical structure in spoken and written (free writing) form in addition to the familiar multiple choice gap fill exercises. Eventually this local teacher called a meeting with the students who all endorsed Bridget's teaching methods and said that the method she was using had resulted in them being able to use language more confidently than they had before. Like Mie Tha Lah, Bridget observed that the exam structure of gap-filling exercises made it difficult to assess how students and teachers in training actually used and processed what they learned (Robinson, interview, 13 March 2015).

Becoming a teacher was rarely students' first professional aspiration. However, within the political-economic constraints of the refugee camps, the teaching profession was one of the few ways to earn cash. According to one research participant, if Karen youth had a choice, many would have preferred to work as farmers: 'Because they have no choice and then they became a teacher. And then actually they prefer to work to grow paddy or to grow plants. Because this is their interest, they have been doing since they were young and they are skillful. And then they can even sell their veggie. And then living in the camp, they have no work to do, no garden, they cannot even cut down the bamboo. So, they are just jobless, living like this and they become a teacher' (Wah Paw Lah, interview, 2 February 2006). Also, Scott O'Brian (2008) from the Karen Teacher Work Group observed contradictions between modern education and the transmission of traditional Karen skills and knowledge in refugee camps. The reason for this tension was that Western knowledge and forms of schooling were perceived as indispensable for a better future. At the same time, Karen community members considered the maintenance and development of their culture as important. This was, however, difficult because Karen elders were not invited into the classrooms. Moreover, within the particular context of the refugee camp, traditional ways of Karen livelihood provision were limited and therefore Karen children had little opportunities to practice traditional activities like hunting or farming. Instead, they spent increasing amounts of time in schools because Western education was a requirement for valued camp occupations, such as translator or teacher (O'Brian 2008: 198–212).

During my own fieldwork, I found that in fact, in the eyes of many camp residents becoming a teacher amounted to making a huge sacrifice because of the long working hours and comparatively low salary. Nevertheless, because of the virtue associated with the teaching profession, teachers had a high status in the camps. When the UNHCR started the resettlement programme in 2005, teachers and other educated refugees were the first to depart to third countries of resettlement. As a result the education structure in the camp was deteriorating, and few qualified teachers replaced those who departed. In spite of this brain drain refugee youth who remained in Thailand continued to aspire for post-secondary education (Banki 2013: 142). Educational projects, like the Jesuit education project outlined below, offered some young people education outside camps.

The Jesuit Arrupe Education Project

After discussing post-secondary education in the camps, this section turns to post-secondary education outside camps. In the course of intermittent fieldwork since 2013, I visited an educational project run by the Jesuit Order in Chiang Mai, Thailand. The project was named after Father Pedro Arrupe, who inspired the foundation of the Jesuit Refugee Service (JRS), an international faith-based organization operating with a direct and personal approach to serve communities of displaced people and to advocate on their behalf, independent of their private religious views (Hollenbach 2014). The Jesuit priest Fr. Vinai Boonlue started the Arrupe education project in May 2013. As outlined above, I met the Thai Karen priest who served the poor in rural and urban parts of Chiang Mai during my doctoral fieldwork in 2007. As a Karen, he also felt committed to assist not only the Karen who were born in Thailand, but also all those who arrived as refugees from Burma. During regular pastoral visits to the camp he met refugee youth. Gradually he became aware of their need for post-secondary education. With the support of the Jesuit Order and his own family in Huay Tong, he was able to help 18 Karen students to leave the refugee camp for education at the Arrupe education project. The project started in his home village, Huay Tong, in the Chiang Mai province. There, his family prepared separate boys' and girls' dormitories, a classroom and a kitchen for the students. Voluntary teachers from the local Karen village as well as Thai teachers and international volunteers offered the students training in Thai and English languages and computer skills. Moreover, the village community surrounding the centre took part in the training. Local Karen villagers taught refugee students how to cook local food and build houses. They also introduced them to husbandry—especially the raising of pigs and ducks. Importantly, the refugee students also worked on villagers' rice paddies during the rainy season in May. Having grown up in camps where rice had been provided by humanitarian aid agencies, working on the rice fields in Huay Tong was for most students a new experience and an important step towards adulthood and self-sufficiency. Their daily schedule was structured in a meaningful way. For example, students had classes from the morning until noon. A nineteen-year-old female volunteer teacher reflected on she experience at the education project:

> 'What I enjoyed a lot last year was the students' motivation, appreciation and respect. I often compared it to the majority of the youth at home that doesn't take education for granted. Teaching in Huay Tong was also very idyllic. We were sitting outside; mostly there were also chickens and cats joining my class. In the afternoon we worked together on the farm. Sometimes a student had to excuse himself because one of the cows came walking in the garden. Once class had to be interrupted because some of the pigs were poisoned. The outside, relaxing and natural environment had a positive effect on myself as well as the students' (Female volunteer teacher, email, 24 July 2015)

Indeed the natural setting allowed for studying and work. After a lunch break, they continued their education with practical tasks outside the classroom. In the village, they typically assisted local villagers with agricultural work. In the evenings, students typically met again to do their homework or practice traditional skills such as weaving. Often, local Karen women who had little time to weave asked the Karen refugees to help weaving clothes. In this way, the students gradually integrated with the local community. Being hosted and protected by a family that is respected in the community and sharing the same Karen mother tongue helped with mutual trust-building. Moreover, practical cooperation at work was easy and allowed for the development of friendships. Indeed the welcome in Huay Tong helped refugee students make the transition out of the refugee camp into rural Thailand. From there, the students aspired to continue their education in the city. When I revisited the students in March 2015, the Jesuit education project had moved to the city of Chiang Mai. There the Karen students continued their post-secondary education at the Jesuit Seven Fountain Centre. Their daily routine followed a schedule similar to the one in the village outlined above. After their lunch break, in the afternoon, students did practical work, such as growing crops in their own allotment, at the Seven Fountains compound. There they continued to practice farming technologies. Moreover, they learnt to use IT (information technology) through the use of computers and videos in the classroom. As outlined in Chap. 2, practical activities have for long been included in the curriculum in the West and in the East. In England, Catholic public schools like the Jesuit Stonyhurst College promoted practical education, arithmetic and science. David Knight, the archivist at Stonyhurst confirms that a chemistry laboratory was installed at Stonyhurst in or around the year 1810. It is generally acknowledged to be the first chemistry laboratory—and indeed the first *science* laboratory —'of any school in England'. Moreover, it is believed that this laboratory preceded any other laboratory in an English school by at least 37 years. Mathematics lecture rooms were installed alongside the chemistry laboratory at the same time. The Mathematical Room was equipped with various pieces of apparatus used for teaching physics. This vivid interest in the teaching of science at Stonyhurst was a continuation of the science teaching that had taken place at the Jesuit Academy in Liège which was forced to migrate to Stonyhurst in 1794 due to the Napoleonic War (David Knight, email, 8 July 2015). This enthusiasm for practical and socio-cultural learning is not surprising given the fact that until 1829 Catholics were excluded from many professions, such as politics, the judiciary and the senior civil service. For these professions a classics-based education—preferably at Oxford or Cambridge—was an absolute must. Therefore, had Catholic students only received a classics-based education they would have remained unemployed. Acquiring practical skills enabled many graduates to find work in trade and other forms of mercantile business (Turner 2015: 80). This situation was not limited to England. As a matter of fact, Max Weber described in his *The Protestant Ethic and the Spirit of Capitalism* ([1]1905) the widespread phenomenon of religious minorities being excluded from politically influential positions by dominant groups and thus coming under particular pressure to make careers in business (Weber 2002: 4). In parallel, Karen refugee students in Thailand were excluded from many professions. Therefore the Jesuit Arrupe educational centre taught them skills they can use to find work such as accounting, economics and marketing. Of course, the transition from the rural village to the city of Chiang Mai also created tensions. The female volunteer teacher mentioned above, noticed how learning changed since the Jesuit education project moved from the highlands to the city. For example, in the city teachers started to use computers and videos in the classroom. It seemed that students were less attentive in class when audio-visual aids were used: they started to listen to songs on YouTube and sometimes slept when video material was used in class (Female volunteer teacher, email, 24 July 2015).

Inclusive education marked the Jesuit education project. From the moment of its inception, the project accepted girls and boys of different religions and citizenship status. Moreover, the project was open to young people with disabilities. As UNESCO Bangkok pointed out, young people with various needs who are kept in 'special' programmes and 'special' institutions run the risk of remaining excluded from mainstream society in the long term (UNESCO 2014). In a similar way, the Jesuits' education project included a physically disabled boy: in 2013, a 16-year-old Thai Karen boy, was living with the students. Since the age of three, the boy has been paralysed and has never had a chance to access school for formal primary or secondary education. He briefly attended a handicapped learning centre in Chiang Mai. However, after only two months he had to leave the school because of an infection in one of his paralysed legs. After a month in the hospital, the boy said he preferred not to return to the special needs centre because he did not understand Thai sufficiently to follow the instructions because they were not provided in his mother tongue, Karen. Moreover, Chai became the victim of bullying when other students tried to strip him of his clothes and rob him of his money. For this reason, the Jesuits asked the refugee students at the education centre whether they would be happy to accept a disabled boy among them which they did. The idea behind this was to teach students to live in community with the disabled. A 20-year-old male volunteer teacher from Argentina confirmed a strong sense of community that marked the Jesuit education project: 'I had experience and training in youth work, but never out of my country. (…) Based on past experience, I was expecting much more hostile conditions from the students, because I knew what they had passed. But I met a group of people who received me with a kind smile from the beginning, and made me feel part of their community; I was taught to live in the community. My richer experience was definitely derived from the classroom, where I learned another way of living and enriching my interpersonal skills. More than a group of students, I left behind in Chiang Mai a group of Friends' (Male volunteer teacher, email, 13 July 2015). So, although he previously worked with youth in difficult circumstances, his experience so far centred on young people growing up in the urban slums of Buenos Aires. The challenge of working with rural refugees was new to him. He regularly taught students computer skills, but found himself learning so much more from them about community life once he and the students met outside the classroom.

Sensitivity to individuals' life trajectories, including the suffering associated with war and displacement characterize this educational project. For example, in February 2015, girls and boys visited their home villages in Burma to spend time with their families and to discern with their communities the next step in their individual lives. So, for the duration of one month between January and February 2015 the group returned to Burma. They first travelled to the internally displaced village Etuta where they helped carry wood for the construction of a hospital building. They stayed one night before carrying on to their home villages. The visits were indeed very memorable for all the students. When I met them after their return in March 2015, the boys and girls shared their home visit memories:

> 'When I arrived there I was very happy with my family. Then all my nieces and nephews came close to me with happiness. Also my oldest brother came back to visit my mother with his wife but I didn't see my youngest sister. Because she went to Tau Oo to study. When I stayed there I helped my mother to find firewood and to make the roof, sometimes I built the house' (Ta Tha Hso, essay, 25 March 2015).

Another student noted:

> 'I was so happy to see my relatives but also so sad because I could not see my grandfather. I knew that he passed away' (Barbara, essay 25 March 2015).

And Lah Ki described his return to his home village emphasizing the importance of sharing work and cultural activities with the people in the village:

> 'When I arrived at home I saw my family and we had enough happy (time) at home. When I stayed at home, I went to work cutting trees and bamboo. I also did some farming, So, I tried to help my family with anything I can do and anything they need. Sometimes, when I was free I hunted animals in the jungle and sometimes caught fishes in the river. On another day I went to the Karen Revolution Day. I saw many people coming there. There was also a beautiful view. So, I was very happy to be in my village. It was a good experience to be back' (Lah Ki, essay, 25 March 2015).

Also, Htoo Ku highlights the relevance of working and celebrating together:

> 'On 22 January 2015 I arrived at my home and my family was very happy to see me and I was also happy to see them. When I arrived at my home, I saw that my village location had changed, especially the people in my village. They made a big road for their transportation. They rode motorcycles and people also developed (their way of) working. I had to visit my village one month .The first week I stayed at home to weave shirts for my brother's wedding. The second week I prepared food and participated in my brother's wedding. The third week I stayed at home to help my family and sometimes I went to the forest to collect vegetables. The fourth week I went to another place to visit my grandparents and went to school to take their pictures' (Htoo Ku, essay, 25 March 2015).

Common themes of the essays are happiness at being reunited with the family, but also missing family members who have not been there, like Ta Tha Hso's sister who migrated for education or Barbara's grandfather who passed away. In their essays, the students mentioned an eagerness to participate in intergenerational working activities, like farming, wood cutting, hunting, weaving and farming. Some of them also noted changes in village development. Returning to their home villages allowed students to see the concrete needs of their families and communities. And indeed one girl decided to stay with her family and care for her ageing relatives. The others returned after one month to Chiang Mai to continue their education at the Jesuit Arrupe education project.

Life Course Aspirations

Educational institutions like Post Ten Schools inside camps as well as the Jesuit Arrupe education project outside camps had the objective to provide post-secondary education for Karen refugee youth. This need for higher education corresponds with refugees' life course aspirations. Indeed like their peers around the world, ethnic minority youth from Burma had aspirations for their adult lives. Obviously, their aspirations were shaped by their socio-cultural and political-economic context as well as the historical experience of conflict and displacement in Burma. Young refugees themselves distinguished three types of refugee youth depending on where they were born and raised. First, there were those born in Burma who came to stay in Thai refugee camps; those born in the camps and living in the camp; and those born in the camp but living outside in Thailand. According to one research participant, the first group had no friends in Thailand and aspired to return to Burma after having received enough education. By contrast, the second group never saw their parents or grandparents' villages in rural Burma. These young people often had no idea of what life outside the camps was like. They were used to receiving food and education for free. Girls who were born in the camps were ignorant about the scarcity of education in Burma. They were more content with the camp-based school education and did not aspire for post-secondary education outside camps. Therefore, compared with those who arrived as teenagers in the camps, girls who were born there married earlier. A third group of youth was also born in the camps, but developed the aspiration to study outside at Thai universities. There, they usually underwent a lot of change, wearing makeup, jeans and short skirts (Moebue, interview, 2 February 2006). At the time of this interview, Moebue was a student at the Karenni Student Development Programme (KSDP), a UK-based charity in support of refugee education inside and outside refugee camps. Studying at KSDP, Moebue developed the aspiration to study at University. And, as outlined in Chap. 7, made the transition to the UK where in 2012 she graduated with a nursing degree. When I met her again in 2015, she had already obtained British citizenship and with the help of KSDP opened a clinic in her home village in Kayah State of Burma. In addition to her medical work in Kayah State, she had also assumed responsibility for her family as she is the eldest and the most educated of her siblings.

Clearly, whether or not young refugees access education impacts on their timing of marriage, child birth and future adult occupations. This resonates with the data gathered during participatory research exercises at the Jesuit education project. I encouraged research participants to draw life course lines and reflect about the important moments in the past, present and future lives. These drawings elucidated the important role of education at different stages in young people's lives, ranging from their homeland in the Karen State of Burma, to the refugee camps in Thailand as well as recent locations of local integration in Huay Tong village, in the Chiang Mai province.

As outlined in the drawing below, students said they would like to work in professions related to politics, medicine, and education. They thought working in these fields would allow them to gather knowledge and expertise for their future lives in Burma. Through their jobs, young people in this study aspired to support the peace and reconciliation processes in Burma, strengthen their communities and support their families. Whilst acknowledging young peoples' eagerness to study for professional work, it is important to bear in mind that research participants grew up in a context where displacement has turned into a permanent condition. In this respect the author agrees with Boonlue (2012) who suggests that displacement is not only about the need to change geographical location, but also about socio-cultural belonging and identity; an internal struggle of individuals to search for another self as well as for a better condition in life. The drawings below illustrate this point.

Loo Shwe (Fig. 6.1) was born in 1990. In 1997 he started primary school in his village. The village school was very basic, made out of bamboo and wood. The school space also served as a church. There was a real lack of teaching material and students used small blackboards to practise reading and writing. Loo Shwe recalled that every year the village community faced armed clashes with the Burmese (SPDC—State Peace and Development Council) soldiers who burnt villages, churches and schools, raped women and killed civilians. At the left hand side in the lower part of his life course drawing (Fig. 6.1) Loo Shwe recounted the painful memory of Burmese soldiers burning his village in 1998. The attack caused Loo Shwe and his family to flee deep into the jungle. While fleeing Loo Shwe lost two siblings in one week. This is expressed at the centre of his life course drawing, where we see the bodies of two crossed out children. Underneath, Loo Shwe wrote in fairly good English: 'My family fulfil of broken heart because my brother and sister fly in heaven at the same time'. Eventually, Loo Shwe's family ran out of rice. As a consequence, they decided to cross the border

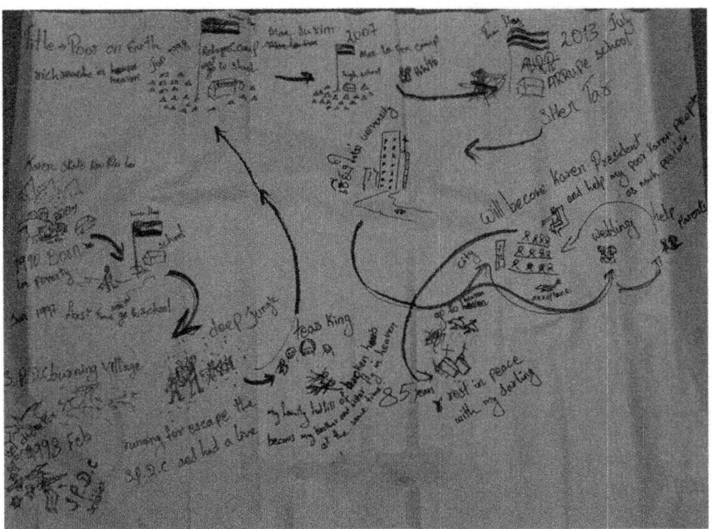

Fig. 6.1 Loo Shwe's life course drawing, December 2013

into Thailand where they found food and shelter in a refugee camp. After one month the family relocated to another refugee camp. Loo Shwe started attending camp school and remembers: 'I really realised that, the education in the refugee camp was better than in the rural areas, because the NGOs supported the education in the camp. We got free study equipment. We studied safely. There were many teachers in school, high schools and Post Ten also set up in the refugee camp' (Loo Shwe, essay, 25 March 2015). In 2013, at the age of 23, he left the refugee camp to study at the Jesuit education project. At the time of drawing his picture, in December 2013, he aspired to attend university. After graduation he said he wanted to marry. He hoped to return to the Karen state in Burma with his future wife to help his parents and have many children. Loo Shwe thought of returning the fruits of his education for the development of his country, city and people. He wrote on the right hand side of his drawing he 'will become Karen President and help my poor Karen people as much possible'. In spite of this lofty ambition, the reality of Loo Shwe's life is rather determined by the structural constraints he is facing. At the Jesuit education project, he learnt important skills such as accounting and English. At the time of writing this book, in July 2015, Loo Shwe was preparing for an internship in Yangon.

Fig. 6.2 Detail 1 of Naw Mar Tha's life course drawing, December 2013

Details in Naw Mar Tha's life course drawing, too, reflect how much young peoples' past experiences of armed conflict and displacement shape their educational pathway as well as their future aspirations. Naw Mar Tha (Fig. 6.2) was born in 1992. When she was three years old, her father passed away. Mar Tha depicted the loss of her father clearly in the upper

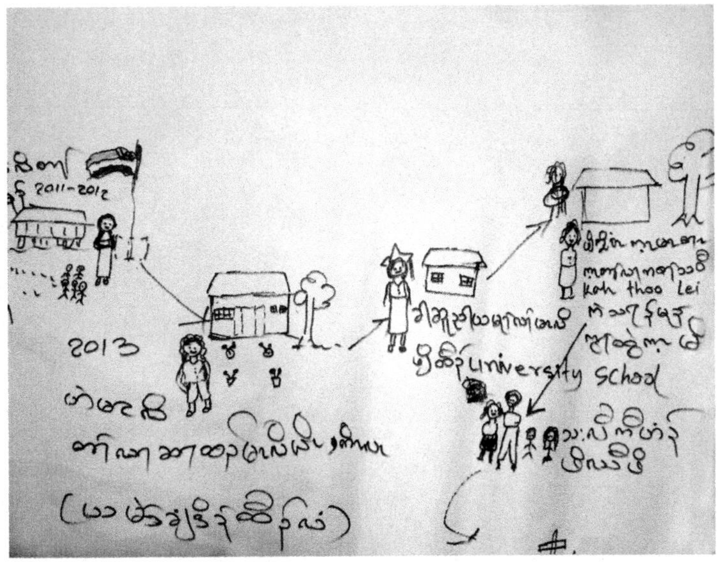

Fig. 6.3 Detail 2 of Naw Mar Tha's life course drawing, December 2013

part of the first detail of her drawing, where we can see a crossed out man at the centre of the paper. At the age of six, she started studying at the primary school in her village. The school building was made out of bamboo and leaves covered the roof. One teacher taught 30 students the four subjects: Karen, Burmese, English and arithmetic. However, schooling was only available until grade 4 and Naw Mar Tha felt that she didn't get enough quality education because there were few teachers and a lack of teaching material. Like Loo Shwe, Naw Mar Tha also remembers the fear she felt throughout her childhood because of the ongoing civil strife in Karen State. While she was at school, she was afraid of Burmese soldiers coming to the village to burn their houses and the school. She was also afraid the soldiers might kill her community. Naw Mar Tha's fear was not unwarranted. Like Loo Shwe and many other children she grew up in a context of protracted crisis. Displacement became a permanent feature of children's lives—Naw Mar Tha recalls how she sometimes had to study in the forest as an internally displaced person. Her educational situation became more stable when she entered a Thai refugee camp. She particularly appreciated the opportunity to study there, free of any fear.

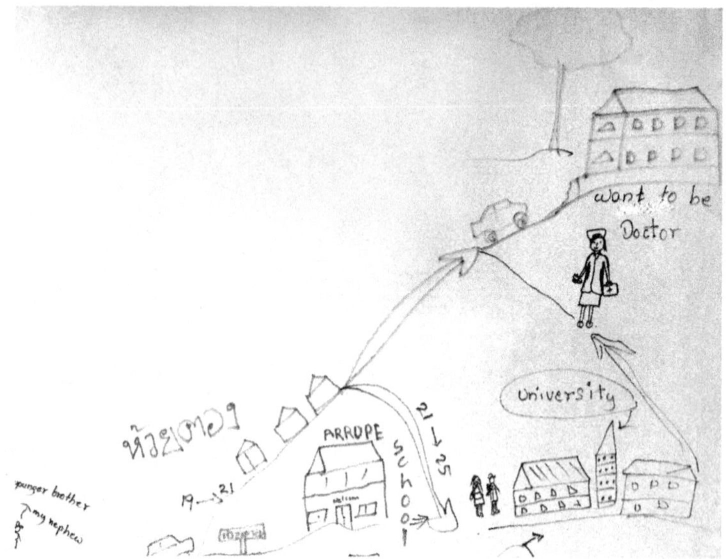

Fig. 6.4 Thida's life course drawing, December 2013

And indeed in the second detail of her life course drawing (Fig. 6.3), we can see a flag in white, blue and red colours. This is the Thai national flag which is raised every morning at schools all over Thailand. After graduation from high school in the camp, Naw Mar Tha returned in 2010 to her village where she taught in the village school. Compared to the time she was a primary student, there were now 27 teachers for 600 pupils and found that the quality of education had improved. Nevertheless, Naw Mar Tha aspired for higher education. In particular, she wanted to study English well and become a nurse. This is clearly expressed in the second detail of her life course drawing. Naw Mar Tha said she would also like to return to Karen State in Burma to take care of her family. At the age of 35 she anticipated having a permanent job as a nurse. She also said she would like to marry and have two children, a girl and a boy.

At the time of making her life course drawing (Fig. 6.4), Thida was 19 years old. Thida remembers that she has been studying since she was 5 years old. The school in her village was small and made out of wood with a steel sheet roof. There were about 30 students. She recalls the quality of education as well as the kindness and patience of her teachers. Although all teachers were ethnic Karen, Burmese was the medium of instruction. Because of the armed clashes between the Burmese Army and the Karen National Union, Thida and her family had to leave their village and move to another location. There, Thida continued her studies in a bigger school built of cement. There were about 500 students, who were mostly Buddhist. The teachers were all Burmese and although they were very kind, Thida found it initially rather difficult to understand them. School days were structured and started with a morning assembly and a flag-raising ceremony. In addition, there was the singing of students' song, followed by prayer in a hall. Physical exercises were also sometimes part of this morning assembly. The high school taught seven subjects: Burmese, English, Mathematics, History, Geography, Physics and Chemistry. Thida studied there until she passed grade 12. She remembers that sometimes there were difficult times because her parents had not enough money for her tuition. Occasionally she had to work to pay for a piece of stationary, like a pen or pencil. She also emphasized how hard her parents worked to pay for her education. Yet, in spite of her family's poverty, Thida succeeded in finishing high school. After graduation from high school she was determined to pursue her studies. At this time, however, her parents were absolutely unable to support her post-secondary education. This was the reason for Thida's migration for education to a refugee camp in Thailand. Like her peers from Burma, Thida found accommodation in a boarder house. From there, she went every day to school at the Karen Adventist Academy, a Christianity-based education project. Soon, her sister, her brother as well as a nephew followed her to study in the refugee camp. They studied well because study material was free of cost. They were taught seven subjects: The Bible, Karen, English, History, Geography, Commerce and Principles of Education. The dormitory provided the students with food and shelter. The students contributed to their two daily meals by collecting firewood and by planting vegetables for their own consumption. Dormitory life included moments of shared prayer, singing songs and studying until late. Thida studied two years there until she graduated in 2011. In 2013 she joined her peers in participating in the Jesuit education project. At the time of drawing her life course, she said she aspired to study medicine and work as a medical doctor. This is clearly expressed at the right side of the drawing. Similar to Loo Shwe, Thida aspired for university education. Whilst Loo Shwe dreamed about becoming the president of Karen State, Thida liked to see herself as a medical doctor. However, the realization of her aspirations was as constraint as for Loo Shwe. In summer 2015, she was preparing with Loo Shwe for an internship in Yangon.

Saw Quala's life story (Fig. 6.5) revealed the importance of the healing of medicine and spirituality in a context of forced displacement. Saw Quala was born in Mi A Lae, in Karen State, the eldest child among six siblings; he had five younger brothers. When he and his family were forced to leave their home village, they moved to Miyani village, where they only had vegetables to eat. Three years later they returned to their native village, but again, soldiers arrived and ate everything in the village. Medical treatment was very expensive and health services very poor. For example, Saw Quala remembers his mother having pregnancy complications and losing a child. From 2005 to 2013, the boy lived in Mae La Mu camp. At the time of drawing his life course line he was studying Thai language in Huay Tong. At the centre of his drawing we can see Saw Quala returning to the camp to become a novice for nine days. This is an important cultural transition in Buddhism. With his peers from the Jesuit Arrupe Education Project, he hopes to continue his studies in order to attend university in Chiang Mai or abroad for a professional career in education. We can see him as a future university graduate at the upper right side of the drawing. Moreover, he

Fig. 6.5 Saw Quala's life course drawing, December 2013

said that after graduation he would have a job, take care of his family and his village. Only when these responsibilities were settled, he said he would be ready to marry and work as educator for the people in Karen state of Burma. He said that as a teacher he would be particularly keen to develop mother-tongue education. Saw Quala also considered becoming a Buddhist monk at a later moment of his life course. Since the participatory research exercises in 2013, the political-economic constraints of being a refugee from Burma in Thailand also shaped Saw Quala's life course. By July 2015 he had returned to the refugee camp where he found work in a project with disabled refugees.

As this chapter showed, whether or not young Karen people from Burma realize their aspirations clearly depends on the structural opportunities and constraints of their daily lives, the support they receive from individuals and institutions. One of their volunteer teachers anticipated that most of the Arrupe students would return to live and work as farmers in rural areas or have a job in Thailand: 'You don't need a high educated job to be happy. It's perfectly fine to work as a farmer or in a restaurant or whatever. I think it's time for them to start their lives' (Female volunteer teacher, email, 24 July 2015). To be sure, students' drawings clearly illustrate their dreams and hopeful wishes for the future. These aspirations contrast with the sober understanding their teacher anticipated for them. Of course, not all students will become managers or medical doctors. Nevertheless, it was important that they had time and space to aspire high before getting ready to accept the real opportunities life has for them as Thai refugees from Burma in Thailand. Attaining this readiness for life is in itself an achievement. The outcome of learning at informal settings, such as the education project, is therefore different than at formal schools. At the Jesuit education project, learning about IT and urban agricultural skills as well as building networks with international volunteers are all helpful resources to start lives as adults in Thai or Burmese changing societies. The next chapter pursues the question of learning within the context of Karen resettlement in the UK.

Notes

1. Hsayadaw Thamanya is a famous Buddhist monk in the Karen State of Burma (Gravers 2012: 358).
2. The other founders of the Karenni Post Ten School were Claire Wildon (Cambridge graduate from Dublin), Mark, a volunteer from England,

Teddy Buri (Former Karenni high school principal and current foreign relation minister of NCGUB-National Coalition Government of the Union of Burma) and Augustino Koon (Former Karenni Education Director and currently resides in Australia) (Mie Tha La, email, 29 June 2015).

Bibliography

Aung, San Suu Kyi. 1996. *Letters from Burma*. London: Penguine Books.

Banki, S. 2013. Refugee camp education: Populations left behind. In *Refugees, immigrants, and education in the global south*, ed. L. Bartlett and A. Ghaffar-Kucher, 133–148. New York: Routledge.

Barbara. 2015. Essay, 25 March 2015.

Boonlue, W. 2012. Karen imaginary of suffering in relation to Burmese and Thai history. In *Present state of cultural heritages in Asia*, ed. S. Nakamura and Y. Yoshida, 21–26. Kanazawa: Kanazawa University.

British Council. 2014. *Burma (Myanmar)—The education reform process*. British Council Burma.

Buckland, P. 2006. Post-conflict situation: Time for a reality check? *Forced Migration Review Supplement. Education and Conflict: Research, Policy and Practice*, 7–8.

Eh Htee. 2015. Essay, 25 March 2015.

Female Volunteer Teacher. 2015. Email, 24 July 2015.

Gravers, M. 2012. Waiting for a righteous ruler: The Karen royal imaginery in Thailand and Burma. *Journal of Southeast Asian Studies* 43(2): 340–363.

Group Interview. 2015. 30 May 2015.

Hollenbach, D. 2014. Religion and forced migration. In *The Oxford handbook of refugee and forced migration studies*, ed. E. Fiddian-Qasmiyeh et al., 447–459. Oxford: Oxford University Press.

Htoo Ku. 2015. Essay, 25 March 2015.

Knight, D. 2015. Email, 8 July 2015.

Lah Ki. 2015. Essay. 25 March 2015.

Loo Shwe. 2015. Essay, 25 March 2015.

Male Volunteer Teacher. 2015. Email, 13 July 2015.

Metro, R. 2013. Postconflict history curricula revision as an 'intergroup encounter' promoting interethnic reconciliation among burmese migrants and refugees in Thailand. *Comparative Education Review* 57(1): 145–168.

Metro, R. 2014. Post-colonial subjectivities in the post-conflict aid triangle. The drama of educational missionization in the Thai-Burma borderlands. In *Post-conflict studies. An interdisciplinary approach*, ed. Chip Gagnon and Keith Brown, 161–181. London: Routledge.

Mie Tha La. 2015. Email, 29 June 2015.

Moebue. 2015. Interview, 23 June 2015.

O'Brian, Scott. 2008. Karen perspectives on schooling in their communities. In *Challenging the limits: Indigenous peoples of the Mekong region*, ed. P. Leepreecha, D. McCaskill, and K. Buadaeng, 181–217. Chiang Mai: Mekong Press.

Oh, S.-A. et al. 2010. *Education in refugee camps in Thailand: Policy, practice and paucity. The hidden crisis: Armed conflict and education.* Background paper prepared for the Education for All Global Monitoring Report.

Oh, S.-A. 2012. Refugee education in Thailand: Displacement, dislocation and disjuncture. In *Education, refugees and asylum seekers*, ed. L. Demirdjian, 78–104. London: Continuum.

Poe Thay. 2015. Essay, 25 March 2015.

Rogers, B. 2004. *A land without evil. Stopping the genocide of Burma's Karen people.* Oxford: Monarch Books.

Sadan, M. 2014. Reflections on building an inclusive higher education system in Myanmar. *British Academy Review* 24: 68–71.

Sister Eugenie. 2015. Interview, 8 March 2015.

Takyi-Amoako, E.J. 2015. Introduction: Education in West Africa: Regional overview. In *Education in West Africa*, ed. E.J. Takyi-Amoako, 1–20. London: Bloomsbury.

Thein Lwin. 2003. *Education in Burma (1945–2000).* Chiang Mai: Teacher Training for Burmese Teachers.

Robinson, B. 2015. Interview, 15 March 2015.

Traedwell, B.A. 2014. Downplaying difference. Representations of diversity in contemporary Burmese school and educational equity. In *Equity, opportunity and education in postcolonial southeast Asia*, ed. C. Joseph and J. Matthews, 32–57. London: Routledge.

Turner, D. 2015. *The old boys. The decline and rise of the public school.* New Haven: Yale University Press.

UNESCO. 2014. *What is inclusive education?*. UNESCO Bangkok. http://www.unescobkk.org/education/inclusive-education/what-is-inclusive-education. Accessed 18 July 2015.

UNESCO. 2015. *Education for all global monitoring report.* Policy Paper 21. Paris: UNESCO.

Vogler, P. 2007. Into the jungle of bureaucracy: Negotiating access to camps at the Thai-Burma border. *Refugee Survey Quarterly* 26(3): 51–60.

Wah Paw Lah. 2006. Interview, 2 February 2006.

Weber, M. 2002. *The protestant ethic and the 'spirit' of capitalism and other writing.* London: Penguin.

CHAPTER 7

Learning and Integration in the UK

Education policies for refugees in the UK have for a long time emphasized integration and assimilation. Towards the end of the seventeenth century, more than 100,000 French Huguenot refugees found a new home in the South of England. Between 1880 and 1914 around 200,000 Jews also found refuge in the UK. The educational response towards these two waves of refugees and migrants was a policy of assimilation and integration: teachers aimed at a faster integration of immigrant children into British society focusing on basic English literacy (Rutter 1994: 46–47). Since the mid-1960s, assimilationist policies have changed to embrace multicultural education with the arrival of immigrants from the Commonwealth countries. The difference between assimilation and multicultural education is that the former aimed at 'compensating' ethnic minority's perceived lack of integration, whilst the latter recognizes the value of students' diverse home culture, and linguistic and religious backgrounds. Moreover, the multicultural approach aimed at sensitizing all children for life in a multiethnic society. In 1979, the British government set up a Committee of Inquiry into the Education of Children from Ethnic Minority Groups. Anti-racism and the stereotyping of ethnic minorities was also an important theme of the report. Under the guidance of Lord Swann a report was produced describing good practices in multicultural education, while emphasizing at the same time that dissonance arises in settings of conflicting social values between ethnic communities and mainstream society (The Swann Report 1985).

P. Jolliffe, *Learning, Migration and Intergenerational Relations*,
DOI 10.1057/978-1-137-57218-9_7

Importantly, although many refugees are also from ethnic minorities, the particular vulnerabilities of refugee children have for long been kept separated from the issues faced by ethnic communities (Rutter 2006: 125). Indeed refugees and asylum seekers are among the most marginalized groups all over the UK. Unlike immigrants, refugees have been forced to leave their home country. Those who spent many years in refugee camps and eventually qualified for resettlement often arrive in their new countries with little cultural or linguistic preparation (Loewen 2004: 36). School-aged refugees may never have attended school in their countries of origin. And if they went to school, their learning was likely to be interrupted by hunger, displacement, war and a lack of teachers or learning material. Those children who attended school in their country of origin often find the approach to teaching in England very different to that in their home cultures, where teaching is often confrontational, students learn by rote, and corporal punishment still exists (Appa 2005: 24). Once they arrive in the UK, educational challenges depend on their age and the place where learning takes place. For example, in a study on how asylum seekers and refugees from 24 different countries access education in four local authorities in England, Appa (2005) found that integration in school was easiest for young refugee children. At primary school, children generally found a nurturing and comforting environment that encouraged them to quickly learn to speak English and to make friends. Furthermore, primary school children's integration was frequently supported by bilingual teaching assistants who helped them understand what was required in class. By contrast, at secondary schools, refugee youth often experienced more peer pressure to conform to the dominant youth culture. When they opted not to be part of the crowed, they often felt marginalized at school (Appa 2005: 11). This was also the case for the Karen refugee youth who participated in this research.

Concerning refugees' higher education in the UK, research emphasizes the value of tertiary education among refugee and asylum-seeking youth. Indeed many refugees and asylum seekers arrive in the UK having already qualified in their country of origin. Often they have an expertise in fields where there is acknowledged shortfall in the domestic labour market, such as healthcare and engineering. However, educational qualifications obtained in their countries of origin are frequently not recognized (Watts and Bridges 2006: 9–10). At the time of writing this book, young people with refugee status and indefinite leave to remain or humanitarian protection, who have been ordinarily resident in the UK for three years, are entitled to apply for the student loans and subsidized fees available to UK residents. However, even for those qualifying as home students, rising tuition fees are a concern (Refugee Support Network 2012: 9–13).

Migration to a new country also affects ethnic identity and the transmission of cultural heritage. Scholars who conducted research with traumatized persons understand that there are non-verbal forms of memory expression, such as physical sensations, and other forms of sensorial, embodied forms for knowledge (Witcomb 2012: 44–45). Indeed among refugees from Burma and Thailand who settled in the UK, clothes in particular have been invested with a range of meanings related to ethnic identity. In particular women's clothing functions not only to symbolize socio-political and cultural belonging, it is also a signifier of the preservation of social morality (Vogler 2008: 203).

Adapting to Life in a New Country

This chapter focuses on educational success by children of Karen and other ethnic minorities from Burma in the UK. At the time of writing this book, an estimated number of 500 Karen lived in the UK. They arrived in Britain for different reasons at various points throughout the twentieth century. While some of the older generation came as nannies in the company of British families who returned from service in British Burma, others arrived in the UK more recently for humanitarian reasons. Since 2006 the Gateway Protection Programme—a cooperation between the UNHCR and the British Government—has resettled hundreds of Karen refugees in the cities of Sheffield and Hull, within the Yorkshire and Humber region (Westerby and Ngu-Diep 2014: 266–267).

The transition from Thai refugee camps to Sheffield was a challenge. While sheltering in camps in Thailand most refugees were not free to choose which country they would like to go to for resettlement. As research participants explained 'you have no choice, you can chose to go for resettlement but you have no choice where you go' (Group interview 30 May 2015). Indeed the Karen were not able to choose were they wanted to go. Once they were chosen for a resettlement country, they had to wait and go through a long process including medical check-ups. Overall, there was, however, little information about individual resettlement countries. America was the best-known destination, followed by other English-speaking countries. By contrast, Sweden, Denmark and Finland were less popular because refugees anticipated the hardship of learning a new language. Refugee youth who went to England remembered that before their arrival, they knew little, if anything, about the UK: 'We never dreamed about coming to England. We only knew about Queen Elizabeth and Buckingham Palace' (Group interview, 30 May 2015). The older generation of Karen may also have remembered Major Hugh Seagram—nicknamed 'Grandfather Longlegs'—who fought with the Karen during the Second World War. Upon their arrival in the UK, teenagers who came with their parents had several months to adjust to their new environment. During this time, volunteers assisted resettled Karen refugees from Thailand to settle into their lives in Britain. For example, Jonathan Saha, who was an undergraduate at the University of Sheffield, used his term breaks to volunteer with the Refugee Council to help on the Gateway Protection Programme. He became involved in a drop-in centre to help improve refugees` English language skills. Neither Jonathan, nor the other volunteers, had previous training in delivering English language classes. The Refugee Council provided a day's training to help volunteers interact with the new arrivals. However, the training was based on the experience the Refugee Council had with Liberian refugees in Leeds. It mainly emphasized ethics related to volunteers' role, such as maintaining boundaries. In spite of this preparation, there remained several challenges related to language, culture and religion. Jonathan remembers the presence of a Burmese translator at the drop-in sessions. However, no translation seems to have been provided in Karen, the refugees' mother tongue. Luckily, several Karen refugees spoke Burmese sufficiently to communicate with the translator. Nevertheless, Jonathan felt that language barriers continued to exist. He and the other volunteers also felt insufficiently prepared to understand Karen or Burmese culture so as to engage with refugees beyond practical problems. For instance, Jonathan remembered organizing an excursion to a local Buddhist centre. The encounter between the monks and refugees became somewhat awkward when it turned out that the monks at the centre practised Mahayana Buddhism, whilst the Burmese refugees followed the Theravada tradition. Therefore, Jonathan had the impression that the support he and his volunteer colleagues were able to offer was found wanting. At the same time he understood the constraints of the Refugee Council, a voluntary organization with many and varied demands on their resources (Saha, email, 1 July 2015).

Karen adults, like Nant Bwa Bwa Phan, also volunteered to help with the refugee children's transition to British schools. Bwa Bwa is the eldest daughter of Padoh Mahn Sha Lah Phan, former General Secretary of the

Karen National Union. Bwa Bwa arrived in the UK in 2001. Until May 2014 she was the UK representative of the Karen National Union, the political organization representing the Karen diaspora. In addition, she was the Vice-Chair of the Karen Community Association, UK, and served on the board of the European Karen Network. Importantly, Bwa Bwa's parents were both educated and supportive of their children's schooling despite being brought up in a context of war and internal displacement. She and her younger sister Zoya completed high school education in a Thai refugee camp. Then, Bwa Bwa and later Zoya both obtained an OSI (Open Society Institute) scholarship to study at a college in Bangkok. The college was St Theresa Institute of Technology which was affiliated with Bradford University in the UK. Bwa Bwa was allowed to spend her final degree year at Bradford University and so she arrived in the UK in 2002. Three years later, after the death of their mother, Zoya also arrived to attend university in the UK. In her biography, Zoya writes:

> It sounds strange, but it was not until I escaped from Burma and came to the United Kingdom that I actually had the chance to learn the truth about what was happening in my country. In Burma, all news is controlled by the regime. Education is limited, there is no freedom of speech; even poets and comedians get jailed if they say something negative about the government. In ethnic areas such as I come from we are also cut off from the news, not by a government, but by poverty and geography (Phan 2009: 279).

Studying at a British university was different from attending college in Bangkok in as much as the Phan siblings were free to talk about their lives, how they had been forced to flee from their homelands and spent years in refugee camps. Bwa Bwa obtained an MA in Education and Development. Therefore, when resettled refugees started to arrive in 2005, she was particularly concerned to help young people settling into British mainstream primary and secondary schools. Initially she and other leaders organized an introductory summer camp for new arrivals. In addition, she provided mainstream support for Karen children at mainstream schools in Sheffield. For a period of three years she worked for a small branch called the Ethnic Minority Achievement Services (EMAS) under Sheffield Local Education Authority. The job with EMAS included going to school with the Karen children several times per week to ensure that they were settling well and to help them getting established. Bwa Bwa typically attended classes with the children and translated what the teacher was saying from English into Karen. In this way, she enabled students to participate in math games and other activities. The major difficulty for children was adapting to the age-graded system which takes into account pupils' biological age without considering their educational background. In this age-graded system, young people in England and Wales attend secondary school until grade 11 (General Certificate of Secondary Education [GCSE] standard) which normally coincides with them being 16. After this young people need to stay in some form of education or training until their 18th birthday. For their post-16 years education youth may stay on in sixth form attached to their secondary school, move to a further education college or find and apprenticeship or traineeship (National Careers Service 2012:# Aged 13–19).

For resettled Karen refugees this meant that 11- to 12-year-old boys and girls who had so far received intermittent schooling in war zones and refugee camps arrived in Britain and were sent straight away to grade 6. Although catching-up was difficult, within a few months the children had done so since they were keen to learn and wanted to succeed. Because of their eagerness to learn, Bwa Bwa found the children's integration into local Sheffield society was quicker than that of the Karen adults. Since her contract with EMAS ended in 2008, Bwa Bwa has seen many of her former pupils growing up and making the transition to college and even university (Phan, interview, 10 April 2015). Like this, school and education became major drivers of the Karen children's integration into British society. Based on a group interview with young Karen people in Sheffield, the next section explores more deeply the challenges Karen youth faced as they started to study in the UK.

Adapting to a New School Environment

Adaptation to a new learning context highlights that school can be both a space of integration and one of marginalization. For example, the age-graded system mentioned above, strictly limited high school attendance to students under the age of 16 years. This regulation discriminates against all those who had had an interrupted education because they grew up in unstable settings. Because of the age-graded system, youth above the age of 19 felt discouraged to attend a government school. Instead, they had to attend an adult learning centre where they were trained in English and mathematics. These courses were mainly intended to help with finding work. For example, Htoo was 22 years old when he arrived in the UK. Before his arrival, he studied at two refugee camps on the Thai-Burma border, including a Post Ten School. The camp environment was not conducive to learning because refugees had to focus on daily survival. There was not much time to read books, especially given the lack of electricity which meant studying had to be accomplished by candlelight. Camp educational facilities were poor, with no opportunities for the experiments that are necessary for the study of science. After his arrival in Britain, Htoo aspired to higher education. However, British authorities did not recognize his certificates from the refugee camp. He remembers: 'They only said we understand, you have this certificate but according to our law you have to go step by step. But we can't do anything. That's why it took me nearly five years to be able to go to university. I finished this year. I can see there is something good for me. Even though they did not recognize my qualification but because I have learned a lot back home it means I just had to refresh because I have been learning already it helped me a lot. What they teach in one year I could finish in 6 months' (Group interview, 30 May 2015). So, because Htoo's camp certificates were not recognized, he had to attend courses at the adult learning centre to obtain a GCSE qualification. Yet, the time was not lost because he recognized in the course content that he had already covered at the Post Ten School in the camps. Post Ten School was therefore a good preparation for college education in the UK.

Children who arrived in Britain at a younger age started attending mainstream high schools. As outlined above, this was not an easy process because of the age-graded system and the pressure to catch up with their British peers. For instance, Naw Esther was 12 years old when she arrived with her family in Sheffield. Before that she had completed grade 3 in the refugee camp but was put in year 8 in Sheffield because of her age. She found moving from year 3 to year 8 a huge jump (Group interview, 30 May 2015). There were also challenges with regard to the new school culture, such as student-teacher relations, peer relations and new learning and teaching methods.

Student-teacher relations in Burma and Thailand are different from those in the West. As explained in Chap. 6, teachers in Burma and in Burmese refugee camps in Thailand have a high social status. For Buddhists, in particular, teachers have a similar importance to parents and monks. Teachers are usually called 'teacher' and never by their personal names. By contrast, in Britain students are less deferential to their teachers. Naw Esther remembers her first day at school: 'So, the first school day, the students they don't respect teacher like in our country, they were throwing paper and shouting and so I was scared and cried. Because I cannot speak the language and it was my first lesson, my first class and I was so scared' (Group interview, 30 May 2015). Thus on her first school day, Naw Esther experienced confusion because she was unable to speak the language. This confusion turned into real fear when she witnessed the unruly behaviour of her fellow pupils and the teachers' inability to keep control of discipline in the classroom.

Peer relations at high schools in Sheffield differ from the way friendships were built up and sustained in the refugee camps in Thailand. In the group interview, Karen youth from Sheffield shared how difficult it was to make friends with their British peers. British culture seemed less open to them than Karen culture. For example, in Burma and in the refugee camps, they used to visit each other freely. Htoo recalled: 'We are all the same and we do respect our guests. In our culture we don't have strangers. Because in this country if you come to school and you are new, all of the students have been told by the teacher not to speak to strangers. But in our culture there are no strangers. We all welcome as our guests' (Group interview, 30 May 2015) and Naw Mu added: 'When I came here I felt lonely. I found it really different. Because in the camp we welcomed all the guests, we felt so happy. But here it is a bit strange. It is different' (Group interview, 30 May 2015). So, whilst in Karen culture, young people visit each other's households, the young Karen refugees were puzzled not to be invited to the homes of their classmates in Sheffield. This seemed so odd to them, that they even suspected teachers had discouraged their classmates from talking to them because they were strangers. Indeed establishing friendships with British peers is not only difficult for Karen refugees. Bridget (Robinson confirmed:

'This isn't a problem particular to refugee students who lack the language. When I was an educational guardian to overseas students they often commented that it was them who had to make the first overtures of friendship. British students never made any effort to befriend them, and these were young people from affluent, influential overseas families. (Robinson, email, 14 July 2015).

Making friends was also difficult because of the different characters and personalities. Naw Esther explained:

> When I arrived I made a few friends, but my personality and their personality is so different. I was a bit quiet and they are so loud and stuff. Normally they skip school, so they asked me to skip school. They don't go to the lesson and sometimes they asked me to go with them and I was to say "no because I am scared of my dad. I don't want to get into trouble with my dad". So I

did not go and we stopped being friends. Or sometimes they went to smoke and they asked me to go with them but I told them no because I don't like the smell of the smoke (Group interview, 30 May 2015).

Indeed teenagers' drinking and smoking are frowned upon in Karen culture. In Britain, however, going to pubs and clubs forms part of popular British youth culture. Accordingly, when British teenagers invited their Karen classmates to go out at night, the young Karen people faced a dilemma because they knew their parents would not be happy with them participating in nocturnal revelry: 'Especially here if you want to make a friend, mostly they go and meet each other in a pub or club. But for our parents the pub and the club are very very negative to them so they don't want us to go. So, even though we explain to them, but they are still very conservative. So, they still wonder if we can make friends in another way than pub and club. It is hard for our generation because we have to be in the middle between two societies, our parents' society and the Western society. So, it is sometimes hard to explain to them and sometimes it is hard to be neutral' (Group interview, 30 May 2015). Divergent ideas about acceptable evening activities for teenagers may therefore cause a generation gap. Friendships with non-white British pupils were easier and culturally more acceptable. For example, most of Naw Esther's friends are Muslims from Somalia, Malaysia or Sudan because their cultural values are similar to her parents' generation.

Learning and teaching methods are also different. In the refugee camps and in Burma rote learning was about memorization. By contrast, in Britain students are encouraged to express their personal feelings and experiences. Referencing teaches students to be accountable for what they are writing. To be sure, my interview partners felt that the development of students` self-confidence is a positive aspect of the British school system, even if it might lead to the disciplinary problems outlined above. Through the use of libraries and computers, Karen students felt encouraged to develop problem-solving skills. Therefore, in the general view pupils have more academic independence in the West than in Asia, where teachers do not expect any reaction or questions from their students. In the group interview, Karen youth also reminded me that respect can be a disguised form of fear. As a matter of fact, the experience of war and conflict may exacerbate students' passivity vis-à-vis their teachers: 'Respect is good. But sometimes respect is not simply respect but it means we are afraid of them and we don't dare to react to them even if they do something wrong. It is very hard to change and to adapt that from a new society. For example, during the class, in here so if you say is there any question and a lot of young people raise their hand and like to ask a questions. But not in our country. Even now if you say "is there any question?" I cannot think in any question. What question might there be to ask? It is like since we are young we have been oppressed. So it is not easy to come up with a questions like that' (Group interview, 30 May 2015). Indeed a Maltese teacher confirmed that in the camps in Thailand students also learnt never to question the Thai authorities and to bear in mind they were guests in the country. This even led them to never question medical staff at the hospital.

Karen youths' attitude towards learning was affected by the socio-political constraints of growing up in war zones and refugee camps. Although they are aware that their past experiences shape their current inability to raise critical questions, they are nevertheless eager to learn and aspire for higher education in the UK.

Higher Education

As outlined above, refugee youth who arrive in the UK after the age of 16 can choose to attend post-secondary education at colleges or universities. The young Karen people in this study also aspired to higher education. Their aspirations were made possible thanks to the British welfare system. In an interview, Bwa Bwa Phan compared the aspirations of Karen youth in the UK and other countries: 'Here in a way we have a chance to go to university and they [i.e. the young people] also want to go to university themselves. They are not being forced. So, here young people are competing with each other: "who is going to university?" "What do you study?"' (Phan, interview 10 April 2015). In other words, whilst Karen students in the UK felt encouraged to aspire for tertiary education, their peers who went for resettlement to the USA or Canada had to think more about job choices to support their families. The reason for these different attitudes is linked to local refugee communities as well as the existence or absence of a welfare system. The struggle to live in North America is harsher than in the UK. For example, in the UK, Karen refugees have access to the National Health System, whereas in the USA the Karen have to pay for their medical expenses. This is why, according to Bwa Bwa, education cannot be the priority of the Karen in the USA.

Indeed, the Karen youth in Sheffield mentioned how much they appreciate the British welfare system, in particular the system of student finance through loans and grants. As home students, most of them applied for such grants. Moreover, Karen youth emphasized how helpful the Student Union was for them at high school, college and university: 'The good thing here is even at the university, if you struggle with anything, we have a Student Union, so if you go there and ask for help, they can help you and they give you a lot of information where to go and how to sort out your problem. I often went to the Student Union and they put me into the direction where to go. Because everyone has different problems. But back home apart from the teacher we don't have any help. But here we can go to see different people' (Group interview, 30 May 2015). Htoo studied at the adult learning centre from where he made the transition to college and subsequently enrolled for a Bachelor's degree in Youth and Community Work at the University of Bolton. His female peers also enrolled in higher education programmes. At the time of the interview, one 19-year-old, Naw Sara, was studying Biomedical Science at Sheffield Hallam University. Naw Esther and Naw Mu studied Health and Social Care in Bolton. During their first year, students said they stayed in shared accommodation in Bolton. However, they did not like it much and decided to return to their family homes in Sheffield and commute from there for classes to Bolton. Combining work and studying is also part of the students' lives, especially for older youth: 'Mature students have to do part time education because you have to show that you are working as well. So sometimes it is very stressful because you have to show that you are looking for a job and at the same time you have to study again. But this is better than to run away from the Burmese government' (Group interview, 30 May 2015). So, although they felt stressed because of their solid commitment to work and their studies, I understood that Karen youth were generally happy to be in the UK where they and their families can live free from fear.

College and university were also more favourable for making friendships with British youth. Naw Mu remembers:

> When I came here I did not have many friends. I started high school from year 10. So, it was really hard for me to make friends. Because some of the student they didn't show respect and it was hard to get to know them. They were not really friendly. But then I met one Karen friend and we became friends. But it was not in English and we could not practice our English with anyone. It was really hard. And also in year 11 I got to know one or two English friends and then I started to speak English and make friendships in English. I really developed my English in College. So my high school was really bad (Group interview, 30 May 2015).

So, although her high school experience was not so good and did not allow for nurturing friendships, this changed at college when her English improved. Young people also became sensitive to regional difference in the English language: 'In this country they have different accents, so before uni I was used to Sheffield and North Yorkshire accent. But then when I started uni I had difficulties because my teacher spoke with the accent of Bolton. It is a different accent. But a few months afterwards I was used to the accent. And Liverpool and Chester' (Group interview, 30 May 2015).

Intergenerational Relations

Since I started my fieldwork with the Karen in the UK, I was struck by their efforts to support their communities in Burma or in the camps at the Thailand-Burma border. The young people mentioned in the sections above told me about a primary school project they are supporting through the Karen Youth Association. Through regular school fairs they are raise funds and prepare annual reports for donors. At the time of writing this book, the Karen Youth Association also planned on visiting their primary school project in Karen State. Bwa Bwa also actively supports Karen educational projects in Burma. With her siblings Zoya, Say Say and Slone, she established the Phan Foundation in honour of their mother Nant Kyin Shwe and their father Padoh Mahn Sha Lah Phan, former General Secretary of the Karen National Union. Padoh Mahn Sha Lah Phan was allegedly assassinated by agents of the Burmese military regime on 14 February 2008:

> The Phan Foundation was set up in 2008 the day my father was assassinated in honour for my father and my mother. Both of them have an incredible history in the Karen struggle. In the jungle we were so poor, we had no education, but both of our parents taught us the value of education and that this is what they can give to us. This is why we have to study and learn, there is nothing else they could give us. After they died both my parents had a vision for the Karen people to be free and not to be used as slaves (Phan, interview, 10 April 2015).

The Phan Foundation has four aims: first, to provide education; second to reduce poverty; third to protect Karen culture which severely suffered under the Burmese regime; and fourth to promote human rights. Each year, the Phan Foundation offers the Padoh Mahn Sha Young Leader Award to young Karen individuals who excelled through their community work. For example, in 2015 a grant of 2000 USD was awarded to a young woman called Naw Hsa Moo. Naw Has Moo served as former chair person to the Karen Student Network Group (KSNG), which was the first Karen student organization. Formed in 1996, KSNG represents Karen students from Burma in Thailand. The organization advocates for Karen students seeking educational opportunities and preparation for future leadership.

Political campaigning was another way for young Karen people to use their education for the benefit of their wider communities. For example, at the time of writing this book, Bwa Bwa's sister Zoya worked for Burma Campaign UK raising awareness of the difficult situation in Burma, for instance by organizing meetings of the Burma All Party Parliamentary Group. These meetings were hosted by Baroness Kinnock and brought together scholars, diplomats, activists and policymakers with an interest in Burmese affairs. In her autobiography, *Little Daughter* (2009), Zoya described her and Bwa Bwa's journeys from the remote rural areas in Karen State to the refugee camps in Thailand, to the university in Bangkok and from there to the UK, where the two sisters successfully claimed asylum.

There are also others who arrived in the UK and then had to claim asylum. For example, the Karen Sister Eugenie, mentioned in the previous chapter, was born in 1959 and arrived in 2000 in the UK because her congregation in Burma—the St Paul Sisters—sent her to study English. She thought she would return after two years, but for political reasons she was unable to return to Burma. Exiled from her home country, she started to work in the parish of Bicester where she assisted the parish priest and attended to the sick and elderly. In addition, Sister Eugenie also enrolled in a four-year course for a certificate in Counselling and Psychotherapy from Westminster Pastoral Foundation. The course took place in London on Tuesday and Friday evenings. After the class ended at 9 pm, Sister Eugenie returned to Oxford on the Oxford Tube coach. Sister Eugenie worked hard to pay her course fees—often as a domestic worker in wealthy households in Oxford. In spite of all the hardship, the pastoral education was very rewarding. It allowed Sister Eugenie to network with other ministers of different Christian denominations. The training in Counselling and Psychotherapy now allows her to counsel young Burmese people from different ethnic groups such as the Shan, Karen and Rakhine. Counselling takes places during weekends when youth come from different places to meet Sister Eugenie at Our Lady of Light Parish in Long Crendon (Sister Eugenie, interview, 8 March 2015).

The healing of war-affected Burmese people is also the aspiration of Moebue, the young Karenni woman introduced in Chap. 6. Moebue arrived in the UK in October 2006 where she volunteered for one year with the charity Karenni Student Development Programme (KSDP). During this time, she found out that the camp authorities in Thailand had cancelled her refugee camp registration and as she could neither return to Thailand nor Burma. She was granted asylum and temporary leave to remain in the UK for five years. During this period she took an Access to Nursing Course at Kingston College. At the same time she continued to work with the charity KSDP to raise money and awareness about Burma. After graduating from Kingston College, Moebue applied to many universities. Like her peers in Sheffield, she struggled because her Burmese and refugee educational certificates were not accredited. Only Greenwich University offered her a place to study nursing. Moebue started studying there in 2009 and eventually graduated with distinction in 2012. Reflecting on her experience of higher education Moebue said: 'It was difficult because I never used to write essays or produce paper work. I really struggled with essays. I also had to work a lot on other things. I had to be well prepared' (Moebue, interview, 23 June 2015). Moebue had to practise what she had started to learn about essay writing during her post-secondary education as a refugee student in Thailand. When she qualified with a nursing diploma, she started to work in Kingston Hospital until she heard of her father's death in November 2013. By then, Moebue was already a British citizen, so she decided to return to her country to do something to help people like her father and mother and all the others who had died unnecessarily at a very young age. The project she had in mind was to open a clinic in her home village. Moebue used her connections with KSDP for fundraising activities in support of the Caring Star Clinic in Burma's Karenni State. Now, when she returns to Burma as a British citizen, she has to disguise herself in poor clothing and cross the border from Thailand as she did in the past when she was a refugee. Because of a constant concern for her security, Moebue cannot stay too long in one place but travels between villages and towns, often in the company of a mobile health teams. Having a rigorous training in British nursing skills certainly helps Moebue as she carries out her strenuous work: 'Going to school here helped me to think a lot and to reflect about my experience. If I reflect I can think what way to do, which way is the better. So, it helps me to reflect. And also how to connect with the people. (…) I think the experience here [in the UK] has changed me. Here people have a right to choose. There, there is nothing. This helped me to think' (Moebue, interview, 23 June 2015). Actually, the ability to reflect about one's actions is very important. In the absence of trained doctors, local people often ask Moebue how to treat a disease. The medical equipment is limited to basic items and Moebue has to apply her own knowledge and resources to heal infections and prevent diseases such as diarrhoea, fever and malaria. Especially when there are accident cases a sound reflection is necessary to quickly determine how to act with limited equipment and without protective gear like hand gloves (Moebue, interview, 23 June 2015). Moebue continues to travel between Burma and the UK for her ongoing development of nursing skills, but also for fundraising events and to give talks. In a personal message on the leaflet about The Caring Stars Clinic, Moebue addresses donors:

> Thank you so much everyone for supporting my clinic with all your donations. It means so much to me to know that my many friends in the UK are working so hard to help the very poor people in my village. When I live in Karenni, my life is so very different to that in the UK. I miss warm showers and Yorkshire tea, but although at times the task ahead of me seems overwhelming, I am very happy to be able to pass on my good fortune to others less fortunate. Thank you everybody. Moebue xx.

Bwa Bwa, Zoya, Sister Eugenie and Moebue grew up at different locations and times in Burma. While Sister Eugenie arrived directly from Burma to study in England, the three younger women spent years in Thai refugee camps before reaching the UK. In spite of their different experiences and backgrounds, they all share the same respect for the importance of education. This value has been communicated to them by their parents from early childhood on. Indeed Bwa Bwa, Zoya and Sister Eugenie's parents were all educated and likewise very supportive of their daughters' education. Moebue also emphasized how important her mother's education was for her own schooling. In all these cases, voluntary as well as involuntary migration shaped these women' s learning processes. Through their education at different sites they felt empowered to return knowledge and practice to other exiled people from Burma as well as to communities inside Burma. To be sure, British citizenship helped them to act on behalf of others, especially those in refugee camps in Thailand or other sites of internal displacement in Burma, their country of origin.

The young Karen people in Sheffield also value education in their lives. Compared to their parents' and grandparents' generations, they had the chance to finish their secondary education and aspired for tertiary education at colleges and universities in the UK. They made their educational transitions in unstable war zones, within the confines of refugee camps as well as in neoliberal British society. Navigating these diverse settings requires the skill to adapt to different settings and methods of learning. A firm belief in the value of education certainly gives meaning to Karen youth's learning processes and helps them to engage with challenges and difficulties as they arise. To be sure, valuing education comes from their parents. Although the parents' schooling was often shorter than their children's, they sincerely valued and supported their daughters' and sons' educational pathways. Passing on the gift of education to the next generation is also an aspiration of Karen youth who participated in this study. Intergenerational transmission of knowledge and skills can take various forms such as fundraising for primary school projects in Karen State in Burma, awarding of outstanding contributions to Karen education, pastoral care and counselling as well as medical training.

Clothes as Symbols of Cultural Belonging

As mentioned above, for ethnic refugees from Burma, clothes and fashion have a particular function in evoking ethnic and national belonging. This holds true of ethnic refugees from Burma in refugee camps in Thailand as well as for those who migrated from Thailand to third countries of resettlement, like the UK.

Even in the constraints of refugee camps, ethnic refugees from Burma place high value on clothing as a signifier of cultural identity and national belonging. Inside the refugee camps at the Thai-Burma border, young people typically wore their homespun clothes, especially on feast days. In addition, the camp schools designated one day of the week in which traditional dress should be worn (McConnachie 2014: 51). As a matter of fact, material culture and aesthetics can help displaced persons to make sense of everyday life in their new refugee existence. In the Thai refugee camps, female dress, in particular, established a connection to the past while embodying continuity of tradition into the present. Knowledge about types and characteristics of female clothing and the fabrics used is treated as cultural knowledge worthy of preservation and dissemination. Older women are especially prolific and competent weavers, able to pass on their cultural heritage to younger generations (Dudley 2010: 92–93).

Outside camps, the Karen refugees are more circumspect about their choice of clothing. Depending on location, clothing has different political implications. For example, in her biography, Zoya Phan (2009) noted that her clothes changed value when she moved from Mae La camp to Bangkok.

Although, as outlined above, she was supported by an Open Society Scholarship for higher studies at St Theresa Institute of Technology, Zoya, like thousands of other Burmese refugees in Thailand, neither had legal papers nor an identity card. Predictably, she faced discrimination by Thai citizens. As a result of this fear, like the school children described in Chap. 5, she felt the need to conceal her ethnic identity and Burmese origins through adapting a nickname that sounded Thai and through changing her appearance: 'I tried make myself look "Thai". I wore trousers, not the traditional Karen longyi that I used to. I cut my hair in a short, Thai-style bob' (Phan 2009: 238). When Zoya started an internship at a telecom company she, again, adapted to the style all the women were wearing: 'I needed to buy myself a smart jacket and skirt, a blouse and high heels. All the women at Telecomasia wore high heels, so I would have to do likewise' (Phan 2009: 245).

In the UK, Karen clothes are important markers of socio-political identity and memory. The Karen wear them at different festive occasions, such as the Karen New Year. However, the dress-code seems more open to individuality than in Thailand or Burma. Participant observation during fieldwork in Sheffield and London confirmed that Karen children and adults continue to wear their homespun clothes at festive occasions like the Karen New Year. The Karen New Year is celebrated internationally and marks the first day of the month of Pyathoe in the Karen calendar. In Southeast Asia, the rice harvest is completed in the period leading to Pyathoe, and according to Karen traditional practice, there must be a celebration before consumption of the new crop. Because the first day of Pyathoe, the Karen New Year, is not a distinct festival for any religious group, it is a day that can be celebrated by all Karen people independent of their religious belief. Karen New Year celebrations typically include traditional *don* dances, singing, speeches and the consumption of lots of food. In the UK, the Karen communities also celebrate the New Year. I have participated in events in Sheffield and in London. While the Karen New Year celebrations in Sheffield took place at Forge Valley Community School Hall, the community in London celebrated at Woodberry Down Baptist Church. The school and the church were both spaces that allowed for meaningful intergenerational relations, including a well-balanced programme of speeches, music, dances and youth performances of the mythological origins of the Karen and their first migration from Mongolia to Burma and Thailand.

The celebrations of the Karen New Year in Sheffield were very well attended and structured. The programme started with the honouring of the Karen National Flag followed by the UK flag. This was followed by a performance with Karen musical instruments, such as the Tenna and the frog drum. Naw May Pearl Tun, the Vice Chairperson of KCA-UK, gave a welcome and opening speech, then the KYUK sang a New Year Song. The KNU's New Year Message was read, followed by some Don dancing by KCA children and a speech by Wendy Taylor, Representative of the Karen National Union UK. This speech, again, was followed by a dance. This was followed by 'Honouring the wise and mature generation followed by words of advice'. At this point in the programme, elderly Karen, together with native-born British people, appeared lined up on the stage, and were presented with floral wreaths by children. This intergenerational encounter also took place in London where two Karen ladies were honoured in a similar way for all their contributions to the community during the decades they have been living in the UK. There was again some Karen Don dancing before Zoya Phan spoke about the current situation of Karen State and Burma.

Among the participants, the author saw married women wearing *hsei wa* (white Karen shirt) and sarong-like skirts. Unmarried girls were wearing their *hsei wa* dresses adorned with colourful embroidery, as well as yellow clothes with black and yellow coloured skirts. Some of the designs were above the knee, not ankle length. This varied from the tradition in Thailand, where the dress code asked unmarried girls and women to wear a *hsei wa*. However, with their marriage women changed into a *hsei soo* (black shirt) which they wear in combination with a sarong-like skirt of ankle length. The dress code was stricter kept for boys and male youth who were wearing their *hsei gauz* (red shirt) in combination with black Western trousers. Some were also wearing their *hsei* in different colours, such as white with violet and blue stripes. This is also a common practice for Karen men in Thailand. Adult men were wearing blazers that seemed to be made of the same woven fabric. Most of the fabrics are still handmade. Although Karen women in the UK have learned how to weave, they have little time to weave at home or teach their daughters the craft. Instead, they order the fabric from Karen women in refugee camps or inside Burma and it is posted from Thailand to the UK. There, the fabric is sewn into garments by a Karen seamstress and her daughter (fieldwork 3 January 2015).

A 'fashion show' formed part of the New Year celebrations in both Sheffield and London. These were particular occasions for young people to introduce new ways of wearing traditional Karen fashion. For example, men wore *longyi* or robes and the women likewise wore robes or two-piece sets of clothes. Unlike in Burma or Thailand, the young women also wore high heel shoes. During the fashion show, the young people held traditional items in their hands such as drums, baskets and flutes as well as a *thana*, a small harp, with at least seven strings, adapted to several tunings, and generally used to accompany historic poetry, love songs and storytelling. The young people paraded in pairs wearing clothes that matched their partners in colour and carrying the traditional tools and instruments in their hand. The young people walked towards the audience, performed some movements with the tools and then returned to the stage. Naturally there is some controversy around the new variations on traditional clothing. For example, disagreement exists concerning the use of the Karen flag on clothes. The colours of the flag are blue, white and red. Blue symbolizes loyalty and honesty, white stands for purity and red for bravery. In addition, there is half of the Sun with nine rays. These rays refer to the nine areas in Burma where the Karen come from. Finally there is a drum which only men can play. The flag was created during the British Empire and recognized by the British. Controversy arose when during the New Year celebrations, young Karen women appeared in clothes which incorporated the colours and symbols of the flag. One of the performers, whose mother made the dresses, told me how proud she and her peers felt to present the clothes. Nevertheless, some community members later questioned via Facebook (ironically making use of another modern innovation) whether it was appropriate to wear clothes above the ankle in the colour of the flag. The young woman's father thought that this disapproval of his wife's fashion design and his daughter's participation in the fashion show at community events was exaggerated. He also pointed to the fact that it is common in the UK and in the USA to see clothes, even underwear, utilizing the national flags (Fieldwork, 1st February 2015). Intergenerational relations are key to understanding how Karen clothes are changing meanings in exile. What is acceptable and what is not needs to be negotiated between the older and younger generation. These negotiations take place within family homes as well as during community events at public spaces such as churches and school halls. In addition, there is a transnational dimension where Karen of different generations in various countries use the Internet to share and comment on community events at different locations.

While there is less time for the learning of culturally significant skills such as weaving and rice growing, the Karen in the UK continue to value these skills even while experimenting with adaptations. At the same time they are using their education and income to support income-generation and school projects in Karen communities in rural and poorer areas of Burma and Thailand hence maintaining their links with their homeland and culture.

Bibliography

Appa, V. 2005. *A study on how asylum seekers and refugees access education in four local authorities in England*. London: National Children's Bureau.

Dudley, S. 2010. *Materialising exile: Material culture and embodied experience among Karenni refugees in Thailand*. Oxford: Berghahn.

Loewen, S. 2004. Second language concerns for refugee children. In *Educational interventions for refugee children. Theoretical perspectives and implementing best practices*, ed. R. Hamilton and D. Moore, 35–52. London: Falmer.

Group Interview. 30 May 2015.

McConnachie, K. 2014. *Governing refugees: Justice, order and legal pluralism*. Abingdon: Routledge.

Moebue. 2015. Interview, 23 June 2015.

National Careers Service. 2012. *'Aged 13–19' Year 11—What should I do next?* https://nationalcareersservice.direct.gov.uk/youngpeople/Pages/YoungPeopleLandingPages/Year11.aspx. Accessed 21 July 2015.

Phan, B. 2015. Interview, 10 April 2015.

Phan, Z. 2009. *Little daughter. A memoir of survival in burma and the west*. London: Pocket Books.

Network, Refugee Support. 2012. *'I just want to study': Access to higher education for young refugees and asylum seekers*. London: Refugee Support Network.

Robinson, B. 2015. Email, 14 July 2015.

Rutter, J. 1994. *Refugee children in the classroom*. London: Trentham Books.

Rutter, J. 2006. *Refugee children in the UK*. Maidenhead: Open University Press.

Saha, J. 2015. Email, 1 July 2015.

The Swann Report. 1985. *Education for all: The report of the committee of inquiry into the education of children from ethnic minority groups*. London: Her Majesty's Stationary Office.

Vogler, P. 2008. Sleeping as a refuge? Embodied vulnerability and corporeal security during Refugees' sleep at the Thai-Burma border. In *Worlds of sleep*, ed. L. Brunt and B. Steger, 193–210. Berlin: Frank and Timme.

Watts, M., and D. Bridges. 2006. *Higher education opportunities for refugees, asylum seekers and migrant workers in the east of England*. Cambridge: Association of Universities in East England.

Westerby, R. and S. Ngu-Diep. 2014. *Welcome to Europe! A comprehensive guide to resettlement*. Brussels: ICMC (International Catholic Migration Commission Europe).

Witcomb, A. 2012. Using souvenirs to rethink how we tell histories of migration. Some thoughts. In *Narrating objects, collecting stories. Essays in honour of professor Susan M. Pearce*, ed. S. Dudley et al., 36–50. London: Routledge.

Conclusion

Anthropological theory describes how gift exchanges express relationships between people. Typically these gift exchanges are about the movements of material goods (Malinowski 1922; Mauss 1990). This study suggests that the theory of gift exchange also includes non-material gifts, such as education. The idea of the gift of education and the idea of the reciprocity of the gift allowed for an analysis of different forms of learning among the Karen and to relate these findings to issues of widespread interest and significance in the fields of childhood, education and international development. Through the lens of Marcel Mauss (1990) concept of the gift it is possible to understand education as a gift that is offered and received, but also begs for reciprocity. Reciprocating a gift is not always possible instantaneously. A span of time is needed to perform counter-services in teaching or in other forms of knowledge transmission. It may actually take the passing of years or generations to return the fruits of education to others. The findings in this book confirm that among the Karen education is perceived as a gift. Whether or not this gift can be reciprocated is crucial for understanding possible tensions and frictions related to learning at different institutional settings. Therefore, conceptualizing education as a gift allows an understanding of the working of intergenerational relations at different locations. Indeed, the Karen legend of the lost book provides the mythological explanation of unequal social power relations between the Karen and their 'white' brothers. This inequality arises because of different forms of learning: whilst the Karen remained subsistence farmers

P. Jolliffe, *Learning, Migration and Intergenerational Relations*,
DOI 10.1057/978-1-137-57218-9

with sociocultural skills, the 'white' brother acquired the gifts of literacy and knowledge of the working of the world. Importantly, this knowledge was originally bestowed on the Karen, but through an act of injustice taken away from the Karen and henceforth lodged with the 'white' brother. Thus generations of Karen waited for the return of the gift of education. In the meantime, grandparents, parents and teachers passed on to younger generations the value of education enshrined in the myth of the lost book. This holds true even for families who used to live in unstable war zones and camps for internally displaced persons or refugees.

Research findings highlight how the gift of education expresses intergenerational relations at the macro, meso and micro levels of society. On the macro level, the book confirms how sociopolitical change goes together with changing forms of education. Whilst in a subsistence economy children need to learn sociocultural skills and technologies through guided participation, in the global neo-liberal market economy of the early twenty-first-century formal schooling became the predominant space of intergenerational learning. In Southeast Asia, the spread of schooling is intimately related to historical processes such as British Empire building, Christian and Buddhist missionary activities as well as the formation of modern nation-states. Chap. 3 outlined the spread of modern education in Burma through Catholic missionaries since the sixteenth century. In particular during the eighteenth and nineteenth centuries schools for Karen were built all over the country and gave rise to the first waves of Karen nationalism. Chapters 3 and 4 also discussed the relation between economic change and changes in education among the Karen in Thailand. Until the 1950s education was largely about the learning of sociocultural skills, such as weaving and rice farming. These skills were important for the Karen subsistence economy. Since the 1950s, rural development required Karen household to increasingly participate in the expanding cash economy. In order to participate, it became necessary for the Karen to learn the Thai language and interact increasingly with modern institutions and markets in the majority Thai society. It is against this backdrop of rural development that the spread of government schools in the highlands of northern Thailand since the 1960s needs to be understood. The socioeconomic and educational changes impacted on the experience of childhood and youth. Young Karen increasingly migrate for education between highland villages and lowland towns. Their migration is supported by networks of private households and institutions, such as the Jesuit Order within the Roman Catholic Church. The example of the Jesuit Social Services (JESS)

Scholarship Programme highlighted the cooperation between individuals, households and modern institutions. These social networks also speak about unequal rural and urban development as well as about intergenerational relations.

Among the Karen in Burma, the experience of structural violence and civil strife marked the childhood and youth experiences of thousands of young people. A whole generation of children and young people has been growing up within the constraints of refugee camps in Thailand. These structural conditions impacted on learning. For example, in the absence of rice fields in the camps, the learning of sociocultural skills related to the rice-farming subsistence economy was put on a hold. This means that a whole generation of Karen youth has remained unskilled in rice farming, the essential livelihood provision of Karen in Burma and Thailand. At the same time, the structural conditions of the refugee camp allowed children to access primary and secondary schools run by community-based organizations and international humanitarian aid agencies. As it happened, many youth even migrated from Burma to Thailand to finish their education in the camps. International organizations, like the UNHCR, also regulate migration from Karen refugees to selected resettlement countries like the UK. Dissonance arises when elders have no ways of transmitting their traditional knowledge or when children find it hard to follow classroom instructions because the medium of instruction is different from their mother tongue. Students feel disappointed when there is no chance to reciprocate their education, for example when their learning certificates are not recognized and their professional aspirations remain unfulfilled.

At the meso level of society, modern institutions mediate intergenerational relations. In this book, the role of missionaries in introducing Western education and schooling among the Karen receives particular attention. Chapter 3 explained how Catholic missionaries established the first schools among the Karen in Burma. These schools were open to both sexes. Teachers were often recruited from among the local population. Importantly, the Karen perceived the presence of missionaries as unobtrusive, probably because of individual priests' efforts to adapt to the Karen way of life. Education had a primary importance—to the extent that individual missionaries, such as Father Nerini even migrated to different areas with their students so as to combine their apostolic tasks with teaching the youth. Importantly, Catholic missionaries also recognized the value of sociocultural learning and integrated skill training into the curricula of missionary schools throughout Burma. Moreover, Chap. 5 analyses the

Jesuit Order scholarship programme for poor students in the highlands of northern Thailand and highlights the cooperation between individual children and adults, households, village communities and government schools. Case studies exemplify how scholarship programmes and foster families enable poor children's migration for primary and secondary education. In these processes, young people receive education thanks to the donations of local and international benefactors as well as thanks to the generous hospitality of foster families, like that of Maliwan in Huay Tong. Girls and boys who benefit from the scholarship programme have some agency to shape their educational pathways. Moreover, children from poor families have a chance to reciprocate the education they receive through assisting their foster parents and teachers with practical tasks related to the upkeep of the foster household or the school compound. Karen refugees in both Thailand and the UK aspire to study at tertiary level. Whether or not they realize their aspirations depends on the support they receive. Whilst the Karen in the UK can ask for government support and take up student loans, these options are not available for most Karen refugee students in countries like Thailand. Where state support for refugee education is weak, non-state institutions become crucial to offer higher education to the Karen.

At the micro-level of society, educational migration clearly impacts on Karen youth's social identities. Indeed, empirical findings in this book also establish that Karen children's social identities are largely defined by their political economic status. Karen children's migration for education highlights how children's peer relations turn into status relations between Karen children from wealthier homes and those who come from poorer households in remote village. Tensions can be created, for example, when foster children feel they have to work more in the household than the foster family's own children or when young people realize that their idealized life course aspirations are not likely to be realized due to their refugee status. In this respect, my research challenges conventional sociocultural childhood studies where political and socioeconomic inequalities between children often remain ignored (James and Prout 1997). Chapters 3, 6 and 7 looked at case studies of Karen adults who recognized the value of the education they received as children and who, as adults, strive to reciprocate the gift of education either as teachers or through the foundation of educational programmes and charities. Dissonance arises when there are differences between children's home and school cultures or between the social status young people have at different places. In Chap. 5, I illustrated how young people shift their social status during these migration processes in the various locations of the highlands and lowlands of northern Thailand. Childhood and youth transitions emerge as learning processes towards mastery of skills that allow young adults to participate in the working of markets and modern institutions. My data evidence that status is never static but flexible, always depending on institutional and geographical location. It is, therefore, important to understand young peoples' social status in their location of origin in order to evaluate the impact educational migration has on children's identities. Disappointment may arise when youth cannot reciprocate to society the gift of education through the white-collar jobs they aspired to. Indeed, Karen parents encourage their children's educational migration with the aspiration that as adults they will earn enough money to support their rural households. Participatory research exercises revealed that young Karen people, too, aspire for white-collar jobs. However, often their school certificates are not conducive to access the more desirable jobs. In reality, many Thai Karen return to their village to marry and engage in agriculture. Yet, unlike their grandparents' generation, they frequently also earn an income through paid agricultural work at rural projects whilst continuing to work in their own rice fields. Although young adults may initially feel disappointed that their education did not automatically lead to well-paid positions, their school education was certainly not in vain. To be sure, in a globalized world it is important to know how to adapt traditional livelihoods to a changing economy. For example, migration between different rural and urban locations allowed girls and boys to build up social networks with households and modern institutions, to learn how to read and write in Thai and to interact with the majority Thai culture. In a similar way, Karen refugees from Burma experience the effects of the gift of education. Their lives highlight the value of education even in unstable war settings, during forced migration and within the confines of refugee camps. Mie Tha La and Bwa Bwa Phan's families emphasize the importance of intergenerational relations in passing on the value of education. With the passing of the generations the transmission of cultural heritage is also changing. Karen children in Burma, Thailand and the UK have almost no formal teaching in their mother tongue. Young people learn outside school about their cultural heritage. Friction arises when youth reinterpreted the elders' way of practising Karen culture, for example through developing new fashions. As a matter of fact, as young people migrate between different locations and countries, they learn to adapt their Karen culture to the contexts of their lives in northern Thai and international society. And so, the gift of education is used to explore innovative ways to be Karen while living with the different generations in changing societies in Southeast Asia and the West. The experiences of the Karen differs according to generation, gender, the nature of their migration (voluntary or forced) and according to their political status in their place of residency, be it citizens, refugees or stateless people. In spite of this diversity, there exists a shared value of education as a gift. Across generations and various geographic locations, Karen children and youth participate in different forms of learning, ranging from informal intergenerational transmission of skills to informal learning at refugee schools to formal learning in institutionalized settings at government schools, colleges and universities. These different forms of learning serve as a means to access knowledge and to participate in the modern economy as well as to adapt and protect their Karen cultural heritage within changing societies.

References

James, A., and A. Prout. 1997. Re-presenting childhood: Time and transition in the study of childhood. In *Constructing and Reconstructing Childhood: Contemporary Issues in the Sociological Study of Childhood*, ed. A. James and A. Prout, 230–250. London: Falmer Press.

Malinowski, B. 1922. *Argonauts of the western Pacific. An account of western enterprise and adventure in the archipelagoes of Melanesian New Guinea*. London: George Routledge & Sons.

Mauss, M. 1990. *The gift. The form and reason for exchange in archaic societies*. London: Routledge.

Index

P. Jolliffe, *Learning, Migration and Intergenerational Relations*,
DOI 10.1057/978-1-137-57218-9

Printed by Printforce, the Netherlands